FOOD FOR TALK

recipes to rave about

Anne Vézina

Food for Talk
Recipes to Rave About

Canadian Intellectual Property Office | An Agency of Industry Canada

Disclaimer

This book contains the ideas and opinions of its author. The intention of this book is to provide information, helpful content, and motivation to readers about the subjects addressed. It is published and sold with the understanding that the author is not engaged to render any type of psychological, medical, legal, or any other kind of personal or professional advice. No warranties or guarantees are expressed or implied by the author's choice to include any of the content in this volume. The author shall not be liable for any physical, psychological, emotional, financial, or commercial damages, including, but not limited to, special, incidental, consequential, or other damages. The reader is responsible for their own choices, actions, and results.

1st Edition. 1st printing 2020

Cover Concept Design and Interior Design: Steve Walters at Oxygen Publishing

Manuscript Development & Review: Jean-Pierre Martel

Editor: Diana Bruno

Photography: Anne Vézina

Photography page vii: Michel Lussier

Photography page 166: Élise Mercier

Back Cover Photography: Claude-Simon Langlois

Illustration page viii: Andrée Vézina

Handwriting page 179 : Marie Ducharme

Oxygen Publishing Inc.
397 Main Road,
Hudson, QC, Canada J0P 1P0
www.oxygenpublishing.com

ISBN: 978-1-990093-00-5

À Maman

For always reminding me to have faith in life

INTRODUCTION

One evening in Brussels, Michel and I were entertaining our French friends for dinner at home. As it was a spur-of-the-moment invitation to our friends, there wasn't any time for me to plan the menu the way I usually do, so I decided to rely on one of the tried-and-true dinner menus I often serve back home in Montreal. Success! Well beyond the usual compliments to the cook, our guests were intrigued by my recipes and asked many questions. This made me wonder.

The idea of writing a cookbook started to take shape at the end of summer 2018, shortly after taking a road trip to Métis-sur-Mer in Québec, with my mother, my aunt Élise and their good friend Thérèse. During that trip, we tasted local cuisine and we chatted about our favourite recipes. And naturally, we moved on to talk about the subject of food. I started to notice that whenever food is the topic of conversation, whether with family, friends or new acquaintances, the discussion always perks up.

I chose *Food for Talk* as a title because everybody likes to rave about food and the recipes that take us back to our childhood, that remind us of good times with close friends, or that we associate with important events. There are also the recipes that seduced our taste buds or those that surprised us with an unusual ingredient.

This book celebrates delicious food as much as fond memories. Recipes from my teenage years mostly come from my mother Andrée and my aunt Élise. As I developed the first inventory of recipes, I realized that family recipes were mainly desserts and holiday meals. To broaden the selection, I added my favourite "go-to" recipes. What attracts me in a recipe is the little touch that transforms a simple dish into a memorable one.

Am I a professional chef? Absolutely not, but even without formal training, I learned how to cook by helping my mother, watching television cooking shows, being chief cook at a summer camp, entertaining family and friends at home, and staying curious. I also took several cooking classes in Montréal, Toronto, Santa Monica and La Jolla in California. I continue to read magazines and cookbooks that always find their way to my night table.

Over the years, I developed a repertoire of simple and tasty recipes from which I selected 75 for this book, each with a personal vignette. The recipes represent a variety of dishes; some are for everyday meals and others for special occasions, whether they are easy-to-make, hearty, classics, festive or guilty pleasures.

In a way, this collection of recipes will become a family heirloom. Who knows, maybe one day Philip, my son, my nieces and nephews, and my granddaughter Romie will decide to connect with the family culinary history, one bite at a time.

Bon appétit!

Anne Vézina

June 30, 2020

ACKNOWLEDGEMENTS

I am indebted to so many people!

This cookbook is a tribute to my mother, Andrée Vézina, and to my aunt Élise Mercier. Without them, this book would not have been possible. They shared their recipes, revealed cooking secrets and patiently answered all my questions. They were my guardian angels and this book is just as much theirs as it is mine. Thank you from the bottom of my heart!

When I started gathering recipes and planning for my book, I believed that I could do it on my own. I had time and I enjoyed cooking and taking pictures of my dishes. As my ideas evolved, I was preparing several recipes per month until one day, I realized that I wanted the book to be published in time for Christmas. This is when I started shifting gears . . .

In January 2020, my first meeting with Oxygen Publishing's Carolyn Flower, Jean-Pierre Martel and Stephen Walters marked a turning point. Their vision motivated me to collaborate with them and to write my book in French and in English. We discussed the overall look and feel for the book, the titles, the cover page, and the content. I greatly benefited from their experience in literature, design, marketing, author coaching and public relations. Because of them, I dared to think bigger.

It quickly became clear that I was missing the precise culinary vocabulary to standardize recipes coming from various sources. Thanks to my friend Sylvie Lafrenière, I discovered the *Lexique français-anglais de la cuisine et de la restauration* by Diana Bruno. This exceptional reference book became my daily companion. When searching for a reviewer, I took a chance and called Diana directly. To my delight, she agreed to review and edit the content of both books. Diana brought a professional approach to the project and infused her knowledge, rigour and humour so the recipes would be detailed and easy-to-follow. Her contribution was extensive and this book has her imprint all over it, and for that, I am extremely grateful. Because of the confinement restrictions, we had to work virtually, and I learned a great deal from our exchanges. As fate would have it, we are neighbours and I look forward to continuing our friendship in person.

I would like to extend my heartfelt appreciation to members of my family who participated in my project and supported me in their own way:

My brothers, sisters and their partners: Louis, Pierre and Diane, Catherine and Jozef, Élise and Martin.

My nieces, nephews and their partners: Laurent and Leng, Catherine and Félix, Charles and Chloé, Larissa, Benjamin, Vincent-Pierre, Charlotte and William.

My husband Michel's children and their partners: Marie and David, Axelle, Romain and Hélène.

My aunts Marie, Monique and Madeleine.

My cousins and their partners: Sylvie and Michel, Paule, Rachel, Louise and Éric and their daughter Laurence, Renée and Daniel, Marie-Claude, Nathalie and her daughter Caroline.

My in-laws: Suzanne and Jacques, Françoise and Paul, Lorraine and Jean-Pierre, Normand, Colette and Pierre, and Marlène.

When the time came, in addition to members of my family, my friends volunteered to test recipes of their choice. In less than three weeks, 53 of the 75 recipes were tested by several people at the same time, in French and English, whether in Montréal, Toronto, Calgary, Vancouver, San Diego, Phoenix or Brussels. These volunteers took the time to cook for their spouses and partners, children and friends. A huge thank you for your enthusiasm and for enriching the recipes with your relevant suggestions and honest comments.

ACKNOWLEDGEMENTS

Thank you to my friends: Rosemary Aird, Marie Archambault, Dorothée Baczkowski, Thérèse Béïque, Lena Bondue, Catherine Boulanger, Barrie Bradley, François Cervo, Marie-Gabrielle Cervo, Frédéric Chauvin, Donna Czukar, Marie Debono, France Denis, Rosanna Desjardins, Robert Desmarais, Don Drake, Nathalie-Anne Drake, Stéphanie Drake, Catherine Friis, Yves Galipeau, Diane Germain, John Gill, Tony Gill, Bob Gumport, Bonni Gumport, Caroline Hachem, Joanne Holland, Line Lafantaisie, Marie-Claude Lafleur, Sylvie Lafrenière, Isabelle Landry, Josée Laperrière, Marie Legault, Sylvia Leonard, Claude Létourneau, Patricia Long, Simon Lussier, John McLaughlin, Jean-Pierre Martel, Maxime Martel, Éric Mélikov, Hélène Mélikov, Lindsay Moeser, Linda Mollenhauer, Frédérique Piché, Michèle Poitras, Riley Prevost, Louise Renaud, Mike Ross, Kathleen Royer, Marnie Scanlan, Carol Schneider, Tina Sérafin, Paul Steiner, Kyanna Terlier, Craig Turner, Victoria Smith, Marc Vermette, Gary Whitelaw and Christine Williams.

Special thanks to Marie Legault, and her daughters Nathalie-Anne and Stéphanie, who tested recipes during their holidays at our house in San Diego, and to Marie Archambault, my childhood friend, who recovered the original 1974 newspaper copy of the Yule Log recipe and corrected a few texts.

I was fortunate to receive staging accessories as gifts from Romain Lussier, Hélène Cervo, Catherine Friis and Mike Ross, who built a wood surface to imitate a tabletop for the pictures. Thank you.

I also want to acknowledge my Instagram followers who supported me during this journey. Every "like" counted.

I was very touched to hear that Riley Prevost and Maxime Martel, aged 8 and 10 respectively and in their early days of cooking, had fun testing my recipes.

I wrote this book thinking of Philip Macklem, my son. As an adult, Philip is finally interested in good food. Mon Philou, there are no recipes with truffle oil but this book is for you!

I will be eternally filled with gratitude, admiration and love for my husband, Michel Lussier, who knew how to encourage me. He tasted every dish and every dessert and found the right words to suggest a change to a recipe, a text or a picture.

Mille mercis!

Recipes that family and friends already raved about

Paul, my resident chef, made the **Buckwheat Crêpes** and the **Creamy Mushroom Soup**. Both turned out really well and he said the recipes were easy to follow. He actually made the mushroom soup four times already, he liked it so much! Marie

*J'avais peur de rater le **Soufflé aux fromages** sachant que ça ne tient pas à grand-chose pour manquer son coup, mais il était merveilleusement léger et moelleux, goûteux aussi. John a mangé les ¾ à lui tout seul!* Dorothée

Just wanted to say how much we loved the **Cheese Soufflé**! We felt like chefs as it turned out perfectly and was so delicious. We will keep it as one of our favourite recipes. Joanne

The **Butternut Squash Soup** is a fantastic recipe. My partner Neido tried it and said: "Don't change a thing, it's perfect." Donna

*Les **Blinis de courgettes** – un coup de cœur sans contredit! Les explications sont claires et le tout se fait comme un charme. Nous les avons mangés avec les filets de saumon, c'était l'accompagnement parfait.* Louise et Laurence

We tried the **Noodles with Chicken and Peanut Sauce**. As expressed so simply by my daughter, this recipe was yummy! The recipe was very easy to execute and will now be added to our weekly repertoire. Marnie

The **Pasta with Shrimp, Tomatoes and Feta** was fabulous! The recipe was extremely easy to follow with the right amount of detail. Nothing was missing. I would definitely do it again. I liked that it's a relatively easy recipe, but elegant for dinner, with great taste. A good one for cooking with friends. Linda

*J'ai fait la recette du **Poulet à l'estragon** hier soir. Tous étaient unanimes : ce mets est extraordinaire, la sauce fond dans la bouche! On en a « jasé » toute la soirée! Merci!* Isabelle

*À Noël, le **Veau aux légumes** sera certainement notre plat principal. Le fait de pouvoir le faire cuire la veille est très pratique pour cette occasion. Mais nous n'attendrons pas Noël pour le refaire, c'est certain! Nous sommes assurés qu'après l'avoir dégusté, nos convives vont nous demander la recette.* Sylvie et Michel

*Je ne donne pas plus que deux jours à mon chum avant que les **Carrés aux pacanes** disparaissent.* Catherine

I made the **Favourite Date Squares** with my Gramma and Poppa, and I worked hard in the kitchen. They turned out so well that I wanted to eat the whole pan, of course I didn't. I will save them for the whole week. Riley (8 years old)

*Le titre de la recette du **Gâteau aux carottes** devrait être « Best Ever Carrot Cake ». Il était moelleux et pas trop sucré! J'ai déjà envoyé la recette à deux amies.* Josée

overview

Handy Preparation Guide

In 30 minutes

Less than one hour

About 1 to 3 hours

More than 3 hours

Look for these symbols at the top of each recipe page.
They will give you an idea of how long it takes
to make the dish from start to finish.

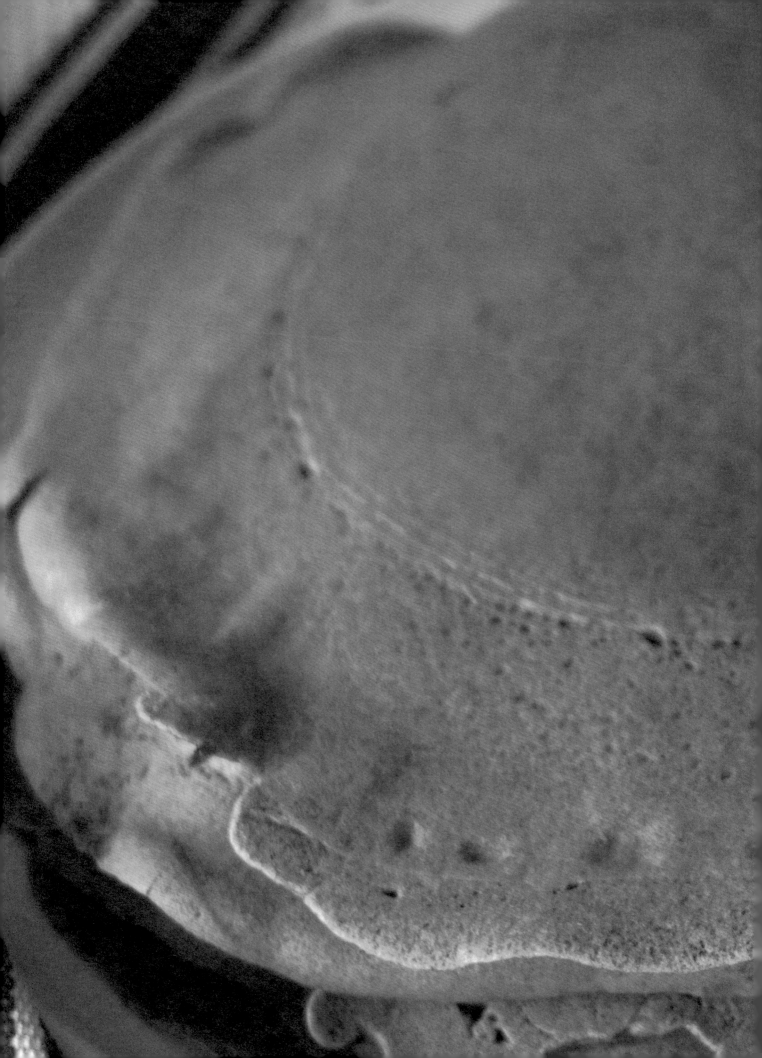

breakfast

For large or small appetites, some healthy, sweet and savoury choices

morning oatmeal

serves 3 to 4

In 30 minutes

Breakfast is the most important meal of the day and it happens to be my favourite meal. For years I would start my day with a croissant, English muffin or multigrain toast with a bit of cheese and jam. Then, three years ago, during a weekend at the country home of our friends Vic and Craig, to be polite, I agreed to have some of their freshly cooked oatmeal. I looked down at a bowl filled with a pale unappetizing mixture and I gingerly took a first bite. Since that day I've never looked back. I now swear by this oatmeal breakast, a healthy choice that keeps me going all morning. I love the variety of flavours and textures of the warm and creamy steel-cut oats accompanied by assorted nuts and berries.

1 cup	steel-cut oats*	240 mL or 175 g
4 cups	almond milk, unsweetened**	1 L
2-3	dates, diced	2-3

Topping choices:

- yogourt: plain or vanilla
- seeds: chia, flax, pumpkin, sunflower
- unsalted nuts: almonds, cashews, hazelnuts, pecans, walnuts
- berries: blackberries, blueberries, raspberries, strawberries
- other fruit such as bananas or mangos

1. Cook the oatmeal: In a saucepan, combine the oats with the milk and dates. Bring to a boil over medium-high heat while stirring with a wooden spoon. Reduce to low heat and simmer for 15 to 20 minutes, stirring regularly to prevent the oats from sticking. Cook until the milk is almost absorbed.

2. Serve the steel-cut oats warm in bowls. Garnish with yogourt, seeds, nuts, berries and fruit, to taste.

3. Store: Cooked steel-cut oats will keep in the refrigerator for 4 to 5 days. To serve refrigerated oatmeal, add a bit of milk and reheat in a saucepan over low heat, or in the microwave at maximum power for 45 seconds.

* *Also called Irish oats, steel-cut oats have a nicer texture and more taste than quick-cooking oats. I use John McCann or Bob's Red Mill steel-cut oats.*

** *Oat milk or cow's milk are a good alternative to almond milk.*

"Green with Envy" Smoothie

makes 3 to 4 Large Glasses

In 30 minutes

This recipe is inspired by the "Green Goodness" smoothie served at The Crosby Club at Rancho Santa Fe, which I would sip sitting by the pool after a game of tennis. Because it's made with spinach instead of the customary kale, it's not bitter. Packed with vitamins and freshness, it'll give you a good start for the morning or restore you after a workout at the gym. My sister Élise likes its fruity taste and makes it regularly for her family.

½	English cucumber, peeled, in chunks	½
3 cups	spinach	700 mL or 150 g
1	green apple, peeled, cored, in chunks	1
12-15	green grapes	12-15
¼ cup	mint leaves	60 mL or 8 g
2 tbsp	cilantro leaves	30 mL or 4 g
2 tbsp	freshly squeezed lime juice	30 mL
1 tsp	chia seeds	5 mL or 4 g
2 cups or 10 oz	frozen pineapple, in chunks*	475 mL or 285 g
2-3 cups	almond milk, unsweetened	475-700 mL

1. **Blend the smoothie:** Combine all the ingredients in a blender and blend until smooth. If the smoothie is too thick, add more almond milk or water. The quantity of each ingredient is approximate and can be adjusted to taste.

2. **Serve** the smoothie very cold.

3. **Store:** The smoothie will keep in the refrigerator for one day.

The frozen pineapple can be replaced by fresh pineapple chunks and ice cubes.

BUCKWHEAT CRÊPES

makes 10 to 12 crêpes

About 1 to 3 hours

I love making these thin pancakes, especially for my sister Catherine and my brother-in-law Jozef when they come over to our house for breakfast. The recipe, which evolved over the years, is perfect for savory or sweet fillings and toppings. The crêpes turn out soft with slightly crisp edges. If you peek through my kitchen window at breakfast, you'll see me enjoying them with warmed slices of apple, shredded Cheddar and a generous serving of Quebec maple syrup.

3	large eggs	3
1½ cups	milk, 1%, 2% or whole, or almond milk	350 mL
¾ cup	all-purpose flour*	180 mL or 90 g
¾ cup	buckwheat flour	180 mL or 98 g
1 tsp	granulated sugar	5 mL or 5 g
1 tbsp	unsalted butter, melted	15 mL or 15 g
pinch	salt	pinch

1. **Prepare the oven:** Place the oven rack in the middle position and preheat the oven to 200 ˚F (95 ˚C).

2. **Make the batter:** Combine all the ingredients in a blender. Blend for 1 to 2 minutes until the batter is smooth. Refrigerate for a few hours or overnight to develop the batter's flavour and allow the flour to fully hydrate.

3. **Cook one crêpe at a time:** Heat a 10-inch (25 cm) non-stick frying pan on medium heat and add a bit of butter. Test the temperature of the frying pan with 1 tbsp (15 mL) of the batter. It should sizzle as it hits the frying pan. Adjust the temperature as needed.

4. For a thin crêpe, pour in just enough batter to cover the surface of the frying pan (about ¼ cup or 60 mL) and spread by swirling it around. Cook until the edges start to lift, and bubbles appear on the surface of the crêpe. Flip the crêpe and cook it until it is light brown. Repeat 10 to 12 times.

5. As each crêpe is ready, put it in a plate, cover and keep warm in the oven until ready to serve.

6. **Serve** the crêpes on warmed plates. They go well with eggs, ham, cheese or fruit.

7. **Store:** The batter will keep in the refrigerator for 1 day. The cooked crêpes will keep in the refrigerator for 2 to 3 days or in the freezer for 2 to 3 months. Use parchment paper to separate each crêpe before stacking them in a freezer bag.

* Adjust the proportions of the all-purpose and buckwheat flour to taste.

Banana Bread
makes one loaf of 10 to 12 slices

Imagine making banana bread with wheat germ! Leave it to savvy marketers in the 1960s who launched a campaign to get home cooks to use wheat germ. This is that recipe, except that I found it too sweet, so I cut the amount of sugar by almost half. Banana bread is very versatile: it's delicious for breakfast, for a coffee break or for dessert. My niece Lara and my nephew William like to add chocolate chips. Our banana bread recipe has become a big hit across the ocean with my husband Michel's son Romain and his fiancée Hélène whose home is in Brussels.

2	medium bananas, very ripe	2
4 tbsp	2% or whole milk	60 mL
1 tsp	baking soda	5 mL or 6 g
⅛ tsp	salt	0.5 mL or 0.6 g
⅔ cup	unsalted butter, softened	160 mL or 150 g
¾-1 cup	brown sugar	180-240 mL or 150-200 g
2	large eggs, separated, at room temperature	2
1½ cups	whole wheat flour	350 mL or 190 g
½ cup	wheat germ*	120 mL or 50 g
½ cup	chopped walnuts	120 mL or 75 g
½ cup	semi-sweet chocolate chips (optional)	120 mL or 90 g

1. **Prepare the oven and pan:** Place the oven rack in the middle position and preheat the oven to 350 °F (180 °C). Butter a 5-by-9-inch (13 cm by 23 cm) loaf pan and line with parchment paper, leaving an overhang on two sides.

2. **Mash the bananas** in a small bowl, and mix with the milk, baking soda and salt. Reserve.

3. **Make the batter:** In a large bowl, cream the butter with a wooden spoon, or an electric mixer at medium speed, and gradually add the brown sugar, egg yolks and banana mixture. Mix until smooth. Reserve.

4. With a wooden spoon, or an electric mixer at low speed, add the whole wheat flour, wheat germ, walnuts and chocolate chips (optional) into the batter until just combined.

5. **Beat the egg whites:** In a clean bowl, use an electric mixer to beat the egg whites, increasing from low to high speed, until they form stiff peaks. With a spatula, fold the egg whites into the banana batter. Pour the batter into the prepared loaf pan and smooth the top.

6. **Bake** in the oven for 50 to 60 minutes, or until the banana bread is cooked and a toothpick inserted in the centre comes out clean.

7. **Cool:** Transfer to a wire rack to cool for 6 to 8 minutes. Turn out the bread, remove the parchment paper and let cool completely on the wire rack before slicing.

8. **Serve** it warm or cold, with a bit of butter or a touch of jam.

9. **Store:** Banana bread will keep at room temperature in an airtight container for 4 to 5 days or in the freezer for 2 to 3 months. Before putting it in the freezer, slice the bread so that you can take out a few slices at a time. Either thaw at room temperature or place directly in the toaster.

* Wheat germ is sold in the cereal section of grocery stores. I use Kretschmer wheat germ.

9

cheese soufflé
serves 4

Less than one hour

Looking for a showstopper? Nothing compares with a soufflé fresh out of the oven. You'd be surprised at how simple it is to make. Really. It's basically just a savoury béchamel sauce with an impressive volume thanks to the addition of stiffly beaten egg whites, and the magic of chemistry that happens as it bakes. It's foolproof if you beat the egg whites properly, keep the oven door closed during baking, and serve it immediately. Don't even think about grabbing a camera to take a picture!

¼ cup	grated Parmesan cheese	60 mL or 22 g
	BÉCHAMEL SAUCE	
1 tbsp	unsalted butter	15 mL or 15 g
1 tbsp	all-purpose flour	15 mL or 9 g
1 cup	whole milk, warmed up	240 mL
pinch	nutmeg, ground or freshly grated	pinch
4	large egg yolks, at room temperature	4
½ tsp	Dijon mustard	2.5 mL
½ cup or 2 oz	shredded, aged Cheddar cheese	120 mL or 60 g
½ cup or 2 oz	shredded Gruyère cheese	120 mL or 60 g
	salt and pepper	
	EGG WHITES	
4	large egg whites, at room temperature	4
¼ tsp	cream of tartar	1 mL

1. **Prepare the oven and soufflé dish:** Place the oven rack in the bottom position and preheat the oven to 400 °F (200 °C). Butter a soufflé dish of 4 cups (1 L) or four smaller ramequins of 1 cup (240 mL), coating the bottom, and the sides using vertical strokes. Sprinkle with the Parmesan.

2. **Make the béchamel sauce:** In a saucepan, melt the butter over medium heat. When the butter is melted, add the flour and cook for 1 minute while stirring with a whisk. Add the milk at once and a pinch of nutmeg. Continue stirring with the whisk and cook over medium-low heat for about 5 minutes, or until the sauce starts to bubble and is smooth and thick. Make sure the sauce does not boil.

3. Add the egg yolks, one at a time, stirring well after each addition. Add the mustard and both cheeses, and stir until they melt. Remove from the heat and season well with salt and pepper. Reserve.

4. **Beat the egg whites*:** In a clean bowl, beat the egg whites with an electric mixer, increasing from low to high speed, until they form firm peaks. To stabilize the egg whites and keep them foamy, add the cream of tartar, if desired. If you overbeat and the whites start to collapse, add another egg white and beat again.

5. **Assemble:** Incorporate a large spoonful of the beaten egg whites into the béchamel sauce and stir gently to loosen it. Then, with a spatula, fold the remaining egg whites into the sauce until just blended in. Pour the mixture in the soufflé dish(es).

6. **Bake** in the oven for 20 to 25 minutes, or until the soufflé has risen and the top is nicely browned. Keep an eye on the soufflé through the oven window.

7. **Serve the soufflé immediately.** The centre of the soufflé should still be a bit runny, but it's impossible to check this beforehand.

* To beat egg whites into firm peaks, make sure that the beaters and the bowl (glass or stainless steel) are clean and dry. The eggs should be at room temperature.

toasts and bites

perfect for light meals, cocktail snacks
or when you've got the munchies

Tomato Toast with Pesto

makes 4 toasts

In 30 minutes

Just as green is the complementary colour to red, pesto is the perfect partner for tomatoes. Inspired by the tomato toast served at Flower Child, a little café in Del Mar, California, I switched up their pistachio pesto for traditional Italian pesto made with basil, Parmesan, garlic, pine nuts and olive oil. And presto, after one bite of this toast, you're transported to sunny Tuscany and its colours and flavours.

¼ cup	pine nuts	60 mL or 40 g
4-6	small fresh tomatoes, sliced	4-6
4	multi-grain bread slices	4
2-4 oz	goat cheese	60-115 g
½ cup	basil pesto*	120 mL
4-6	fresh basil leaves, in thin ribbons	4-6
1 tbsp	extra-virgin olive oil	15 mL
	salt and pepper	

1. Toast the pine nuts: In a small frying pan, toast the pine nuts without oil over medium heat for 3 to 5 minutes, or until they are lightly browned. Reserve.

2. Prepare the toasts: Toast the slices of bread in a toaster and spread the goat cheese on each slice. Add a bit of pesto on top of the cheese. Arrange the tomato slices on the goat cheese and add a dab of pesto on each tomato slice.

3. Serve: Garnish the toasts with the pine nuts and basil. Drizzle with olive oil. Season with salt and pepper.

* Pesto is sold at the grocery store in a small jar, usually in the pasta section.

AVOCADO TOAST
WITH Green Peas and Smoked Salmon

In 30 minutes

makes 8 toasts

In 2010, the same year that Instagram came into existence, avocado toast grabbed the spotlight, becoming one of the most Instagrammed dishes. I came across this recipe for avocado toast when I was flipping through magazines as I was sitting in a doctor's office waiting for my name to be called. This is Jamie Vespa's recipe in the magazine Cooking Light in August 2017. After her first few bites, my niece Charlotte, an active Instagrammer, declared this would be her go-to avocado toast; she loved the flavour combination of green peas and mint with avocado. My sister-in-law Lorraine prefers to serve it in bite-size portions as an appetizer or a cocktail snack.

2	ripe avocados	2
¾ cup	frozen green peas, thawed	180 mL or 100 g
1 tbsp	freshly squeezed lemon juice	15 mL
1 tbsp	chopped fresh mint	15 mL or 2 g
¼ tsp	salt	1 mL
¼ tsp	ground black pepper	1 mL
8	slices of sourdough bread, toasted	8
8 oz	smoked salmon, thinly sliced*	225 g
1 tbsp	extra-virgin olive oil	15 mL
	GARNISH	
4	radishes, thinly sliced	4
	fresh mint, chopped	

1. **Make the avocado spread:** Cut each avocado in half and remove the pit. Use a spoon to scoop the avocado flesh into a bowl. Use a fork to mash together the avocado and green peas while leaving some texture. Add the lemon juice, chopped mint, salt and pepper. Mix.

2. **Assemble:** Spread the avocado mixture on each slice of bread. Top with a slice of smoked salmon and a drizzle of olive oil.

3. **Serve** each toast garnished with the radish slices and chopped mint. Season with salt and pepper. Avocado toasts taste best when served immediately.

* The smoked salmon can be replaced by small cooked shrimp.

ITALIAN SANDWICH WITH EGGPLANT

MAKES 2 TO 3 SANDWICHES

Less than one hour

Bersani and Carlevale, an Italian bistro on Toronto's Bloor Street in the 1980s, listed an unusual sandwich on its menu one made with sliced eggplant. My friend Craig, who adored the sandwich as much as I did, helped me recreate their sandwich. I can't remember if there was any avocado, but why not?

1	large eggplant	1
1	large egg, beaten with a bit of water	1
1 cup	breadcrumbs	240 mL or 150 g
2-3 tbsp	olive oil	30-45 mL
4-6 slices	pumpernickel bread*	4-6 slices
3 tbsp	mayonnaise	45 mL
3-6	lettuce leaves, Romaine or Bibb	3-6
2-3	medium tomatoes, sliced	2-3
1	avocado, sliced (optional)	1
	salt and pepper	
4-6 oz	mozzarella or provolone cheese, sliced	115-170 g
	alfalfa sprouts	

1. **Prepare the eggplant**:** Remove the ends of the unpeeled eggplant and cut lengthwise into about 8 slices ¼-inch (6 mm) thick.

2. **Coat the eggplant:** Prepare two plates, one for the beaten egg and water, the other for the breadcrumbs. Dip each slice in the beaten egg and then in the breadcrumbs to coat it on both sides. Reserve.

3. **Cook the eggplant:** In a non-stick frying pan, sauté a few eggplant slices in very hot olive oil for 5 to 8 minutes, or until each slice is browned on both sides. Adjust the heat and add olive oil as needed. Transfer the eggplant slices to a plate lined with paper towels. Repeat with the remaining slices and reserve.

4. **Assemble and serve:** Spread mayonnaise on each slice of bread. On half of the slices of bread, place the lettuce, tomato slices and avocado slices (optional). Season with salt and pepper. Continue with the grilled eggplant slices and the cheese. Garnish with alfalfa sprouts. Top with the remaining bread slices and serve.

* This sandwich tastes best when made with very soft bread.
** The eggplant slices can be prepared in advance.

tuna melt
serves 2

At lunch time, I often can't decide between a grilled cheese sandwich or a tuna salad. Luckily, a tuna melt is the answer to both cravings. I love the crispness of celery, the sharpness of shallots and the tang of capers in a seasoned mayonnaise with chunky tuna. Top it off with some Cheddar and place under the broiler for a quickly pulled together oh-so-satisfying open-face sandwich for all seasons.

5 oz	canned tuna in water	141 g
1	celery stalk, finely chopped	1
1 tbsp	finely chopped shallot	15 mL or 9 g
2 tsp	capers, rinsed	10 mL or 8 g
2-3 tbsp	mayonnaise	30-45 mL
1½ tsp	Dijon mustard	7.5 mL
1 tsp	horseradish	5 mL
1 tsp	freshly squeezed lemon juice	5 mL
	celery salt and pepper	
1 tbsp	chopped fresh dill fronds (optional)	15 mL or 2 g
1	lemon, zested (optional)	1
2	English muffins, in halves	2
2 oz	sharp Cheddar cheese, shredded or sliced	60 g

1. **Prepare the oven and sheet pan:** Place the oven rack in the top position and preheat the broiler. Line a sheet pan with parchment paper.

2. **Make the tuna mixture*:** Drain the tuna and break it up with a fork in a bowl. Add the celery, shallot, capers, mayonnaise, Dijon mustard, horseradish, lemon juice, celery salt and pepper. Mix, taste and adjust the seasoning. Optional: Add the chopped dill and the lemon zest. Mix.

3. **Make the open-face sandwich:** Toast the English muffins in a toaster. Spread one-quarter of the tuna mixture on each English muffin half. Top with Cheddar cheese.

4. **Broil and serve:** Place the open-face tuna sandwiches under the broiler for 1 to 2 minutes, or until the cheese starts bubbling and is golden brown. Serve immediately.

* The tuna mixture can be prepared in advance and refrigerated for 1 to 2 days.

cheese bites
makes 48 bites of 1½ inches (4 cm)

This is my sister-in-law Suzanne's recipe. I'm crazy about her cheese bites and I'm in very good company. She makes them in industrial quantities almost every week because they're a great favourite at family gatherings, whether we're 4 or 80 people (yes, my in-laws' family is quite large). I'm also treated to my very own stash whenever Suzanne and her partner Jacques come to visit us. As much as I enjoy having an "official supplier", I also enjoy making them myself and ensuring I have a steady supply when my official stash runs out.

8 oz	extra-old Cheddar cheese*	225 g
1 cup	all-purpose flour	240 mL or 120 g
⅓ cup	margarine or cold unsalted butter**	80 mL or 75 g
2 tsp	dry mustard	10 mL or 6 g
½ tsp	garlic powder	2.5 mL
¼ tsp	cayenne pepper	1 mL
¼ cup	cold water	60 mL

1. **Prepare the oven and cookie sheet:** Place the oven rack in the middle position and preheat the oven to 375 °F (190 °C). Line a cookie sheet with parchment paper.

2. **Make the dough:** Grate the cheese in a food processor***, or with a cheese grater. Add all the other ingredients (except the water) in the food processor and pulse to mix. Add the cold water little by little and continue to pulse until the dough is smooth.

3. **Shape the dough:** On a work surface, use your hands to press the dough gently into a ball. Turn and press the ball 3 or 4 times to blend in any dry bits. Flatten the ball into a thick disk and wrap in plastic. Let rest in the refrigerator for at least one hour.

4. **Shape into bites:** Roll the dough with a rolling pin, as you would do for pie crust, to a thickness of about ⅛ inch (3 mm). With a 1½-inch (4 cm) cookie cutter, cut out circular pieces and place them on the cookie sheet, leaving about 1 inch (2.5 cm) between each.

5. **Bake** in the oven for about 15 minutes, or until the cookies are golden brown. The cooking time depends on the thickness of the cheese bites. Transfer to a wire rack to cool.

6. **Serve** the cheese bites slightly warm or at room temperature. Great for grazing, with a soup or salad.

7. **Store:** Cheese bites will keep at room temperature in an airtight container for 4 to 5 days or in the freezer for 2 to 3 months.

*   *Suzanne's recipe called for extra-old Black Diamond Cheddar cheese. Other brands of extra-old Cheddar cheese work well, too.*

**   *For a slightly flakier texture, use butter instead of margarine.*

*** *If you don't have a food processor, use an electric mixer, or work with a pastry cutter.*

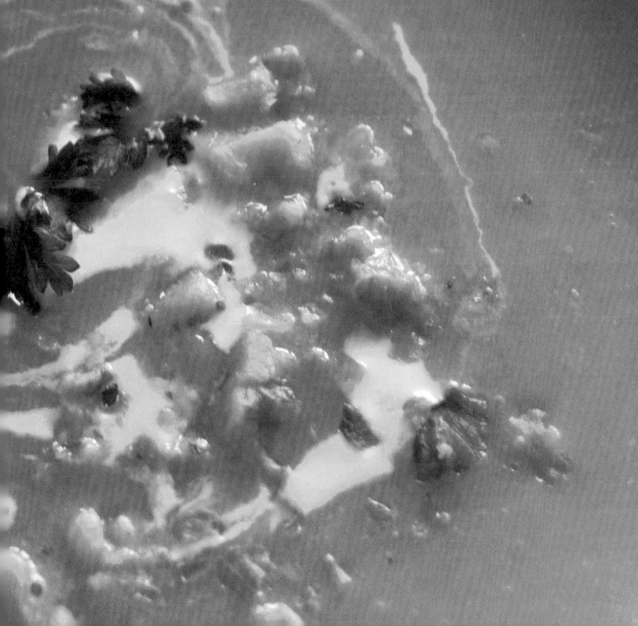

SOUPS
COLD AND HOT, WITH A PALETTE OF FLAVOURS AND COLOURS

GAZPACHO
serves 4 to 6

About 1 to 3 hours

My grandmother Thérèse grew up in Richelieu, Québec and continued spending her summers there after she got married to my grandfather Élie Beauregard. Every summer she would make her own version of this classic Spanish chilled soup. She was an excellent cook and took great pride in her vegetable garden. I can still see her in front of her kitchen window carefully peeling and cutting up fresh vegetables with her delicate seamstress hands. This gazpacho is tasty and textured with crisp, finely diced vegetables and is so refreshing on lazy, hazy, hot summer days.

4	large tomatoes, peeled and seeded*	4
1	medium onion	1
1	cucumber, peeled and seeded	1
1	green pepper	1
3 oz	tomato paste	85 g
2 cups	tomato juice	475 mL
3 tbsp	extra-virgin olive oil	45 mL
1 tbsp	red wine vinegar	15 mL
1 tbsp	freshly squeezed lemon juice	15 mL
3-4 dashes	Tabasco sauce	3-4 dashes
1-2	garlic cloves, puréed	1-2
	salt and pepper	
	extra-virgin olive oil	
	fresh parsley, curly or flat, chopped	
	croutons	

1. **Cut the vegetables:** On a cutting board, cut the tomatoes, onion, cucumber and green pepper into ¼-inch (6 mm) dice.

2. **Assemble:** Combine all the vegetables in a large bowl. Add the tomato paste, tomato juice, olive oil, red wine vinegar, lemon juice, Tabasco and garlic. Mix well. If the soup is too thick, add a bit more tomato juice. Season with salt and pepper.

3. **Cool** in the refrigerator for a few hours or overnight to allow the flavours to blend. When ready to serve, taste and adjust the seasoning as needed with lemon juice, red wine vinegar, Tabasco, salt or pepper.

4. **Serve** the gazpacho cold with a drizzle of olive oil, garnished with fresh parsley and croutons.

5. **Store:** The gazpacho will keep in the refrigerator for 1 to 2 days.

* The quality of the tomatoes is what makes the gazpacho; they should be fresh, flavourful and juicy.

Green Pea Soup
serves 4

My brother-in-law Normand likes this soup because it's just about the fastest soup to make and the perfect dish if you haven't planned ahead. Who doesn't have a bag of green peas in the freezer and chicken broth in the cupboard? Thin or thick, this appetizing soup is comfort food on cold wintry days or, if served chilled, refreshing in the heat of summer.

1 tbsp	unsalted butter	15 mL or 15 g
1 tbsp	olive oil	15 mL
1	medium onion, chopped	1
2 cups	frozen green peas	475 mL or 260 g
2 cups	chicken broth*	475 mL
	salt and pepper	
	fresh mint or chives, chopped	
¼ cup	pancetta, in ⅜-inch (1 cm) dice, sautéed (optional)	60 mL or 30 g

1. **Cook the vegetables:** In a saucepan, cook the onion in the butter and olive oil over medium-low heat for 4 to 5 minutes, or until the onion is softened.

2. Add the frozen green peas and cover. Cook over medium-low heat for 3 to 5 minutes. Add salt and pepper.

3. **Make the soup:** Add the chicken broth and bring to a boil. Reduce the heat to low and simmer uncovered for 6 to 8 minutes. To keep the peas bright green, do not overcook.

4. **Blend:** Purée the soup using a blender until it is almost smooth. If the soup is too thick, add more chicken broth. Taste and adjust the seasoning, as needed.

5. **Serve** the soup garnished with mint or chives, and pancetta (optional). In summertime, serve the soup cold with a dollop of plain yogourt.

6. **Store:** The soup will keep in the refrigerator for 2 to 3 days or in the freezer for 2 to 3 months.

* For a vegetarian version of the soup, use vegetable broth.

Butternut Squash Soup
serves 4 to 6

Less than one hour

It was several years ago, when I was at my friend Catherine's apartment in Toronto, that I first tasted this vegetable soup. At the time, butternut squash soup was not as trendy as it is today. The sweet taste of the butternut squash, its silky texture and golden colour captivated my taste buds. I make this super easy recipe with leeks and chicken broth all the time and never get tired of it.

1 tbsp	unsalted butter	15 mL or 15 g
1 tbsp	olive oil	15 mL
2 cups or 6 oz	leeks, white and pale green parts, sliced	475 mL or 170 g
3-4 cups or 20 oz	butternut squash, in cubes*	700-950 mL or 570 g
3-4 cups	chicken broth**	700-950 mL
	salt and pepper	
	sour cream or plain yogourt	
	chives, or another herb, chopped	60 mL or 30 g

1. **Cook the vegetables:** In a saucepan, cook the leeks in the butter and olive oil over medium-low heat for 4 to 5 minutes, or until the leeks are softened.

2. Add the butternut squash and cover. Cook over medium-low heat for 8 to 10 minutes, or until the butternut squash is softened. Season with salt and pepper.

3. **Make the soup:** Add the chicken broth and bring to a boil. Reduce the heat to low and simmer uncovered for 10 to 12 minutes***.

4. **Blend:** Purée the soup using a blender until smooth. If the soup is too thick, add more chicken broth. Taste and adjust the seasoning, as needed.

5. **Serve** the soup with a small knob of sour cream or plain yogourt, and a garnish of chives.

6. **Store:** The soup will keep in the refrigerator for 2 to 3 days or in the freezer for 2 to 3 months.

*   *You can replace the butternut squash by 2-3 medium zucchini.*
**   *For a vegetarian version of the soup, use vegetable broth.*
*** *For variety, add 1 cup (240 mL) of coconut milk and 1 tsp (5 mL) of curry powder.*

CARROT SOUP
serves 4 to 6

Less than one hour

My recipe for making vegetable soup is as simple as combining a "star vegetable" with leeks and chicken broth. For this soup, I added a surprising ingredient — orange juice. The subtle touch of citrus brightens up both the taste and the colour of the soup. Just for fun, ask your guests to guess the mystery ingredient!

1 tbsp	unsalted butter	15 mL or 15 g
1 tbsp	olive oil	15 mL
2 cups or 6 oz	leeks, white and pale green parts, sliced	475 mL or 170 g
3-4 cups or 20 oz	medium carrots, chopped	700-950 mL or 570 g
3 cups	chicken broth*	700 mL
¾ cup	orange juice	180 mL
	salt and pepper	
⅛ tsp	ground cumin	0.5 mL
	crème fraiche or plain yogourt	
	walnuts, chopped	
	fresh parsley, curly or flat, chopped	

1. **Cook the vegetables:** In a saucepan, cook the leeks in the butter and olive oil over medium-low heat for 4 to 5 minutes, or until the leeks are softened.

2. Add the carrots and cover. Cook over medium-low heat for 10 to 12 minutes, or until the carrots are softened. Season with salt, pepper and cumin.

3. **Make the soup:** Add the chicken broth and bring to a boil. Reduce the heat to low and simmer uncovered for 8 to 10 minutes. Add the orange juice and simmer for 5 minutes.

4. **Blend:** Purée the soup using a blender until smooth. If the soup is too thick, add more chicken broth or orange juice. Taste and adjust the seasoning, as needed.

5. **Serve** the soup garnished with a small knob of crème fraiche or plain yogourt, chopped walnuts and parsley.

6. **Store:** The soup will keep in the refrigerator for 2 to 3 days or in the freezer for 2 to 3 months.

* For a vegetarian version of the soup, use vegetable broth.

33

creamy mushroom soup
serves 4 to 6

Less than one hour

There's magic in my aunt Elise's mushroom soup. And it's not magic mushrooms. The wow factor comes from plain old beef consommé that brings out the natural taste of umami in the mushrooms. It's my husband Michel's favourite soup and it's THE soup that generates the most compliments from our male guests. Nine times out of ten, they'll ask me for the recipe. I'm thinking about Jean-Pierre, Paul, Christian, Yves, Frédéric . . .

3 tbsp	unsalted butter	45 mL or 45 g
1 cup	medium onion, finely chopped	240 mL or 130 g
6-8 oz	white mushrooms, sliced	170-225 g
2-4 tbsp	chopped fresh curly parsley	30-60 mL or 4-8 g
2 tbsp	all-purpose flour	30 mL or 16 g
10-oz can	beef consommé*	285 mL
2 cups	whole milk	475 mL
2-3 tbsp	sherry or freshly squeezed lemon juice	30-45 mL
2 tbsp	crème fraîche (optional)	30 mL
	fresh curly parsley, chopped	
	lemon zest (optional)	

1. **Cook the vegetables:** In a saucepan, cook the onion in the butter over medium-low heat for 4 to 5 minutes, or until the onion is softened.

2. Add the mushrooms and parsley. Stir and season with salt and pepper. Cover and cook over medium-low heat for 6 to 8 minutes, or until the liquid released by the mushrooms starts to simmer.

3. **Make the soup:** Add the flour and stir with a wooden spoon for 2 to 3 minutes for the flour to cook. Add the beef consommé and bring to a boil. Reduce the heat to low and add the milk.

4. **Cook** uncovered over low heat for 10 minutes and stir regularly. Be careful not to let the milk boil!

5. **Serve:** Before serving, add the sherry, or lemon juice, and crème fraîche (optional). Taste and adjust the seasoning as needed. Sprinkle with parsley and lemon zest (optional).

6. **Store:** This soup will keep in the refrigerator for 3 to 4 days but can't be frozen.

* I use Campbell's beef consommé. As a substitute, use beef broth with 1 tbsp (15 mL) of soya sauce.

salaDs

around the world with seven salads served
as an appetizer, main course or side dish

annouche salad
serves 4 to 6

Less than one hour

For fun, I chose to name this salad "Annouche", my mother's affectionate nickname for me. My starting point was Syria's classic Fattouch Salad, and just like it, I also use a medley of pomegranate, parsley, mint, sumac, cinnamon and allspice to harmonize with the tomatoes, cucumbers, bell peppers and radishes. Each bite of the crisp vegetables, cut almost to the size of pomegranate seeds, is bursting with freshness. You'll be bewitched by the mosaic of flavours, colours and textures.

	DRESSING	
¼ cup	extra-virgin olive oil	60 mL
¼ cup	freshly squeezed lime juice	60 mL
¼ cup	pomegranate molasses*	60 mL
¼ tsp	ground cinnamon	1 mL
¼ tsp	ground allspice	1 mL
	SALAD	
2 cups	fresh curly parsley, finely chopped	475 mL or 60 g
1 cup	mint leaves, finely chopped	240 mL or 30 g
1 cup	pomegranate seeds	240 mL or 170 g
1 cup	cherry tomatoes, cut in half	240 mL or 150 g
1 cup	Lebanese cucumber, small dice	240 mL or 130 g
½ cup	yellow bell pepper, small dice	120 mL or 65 g
½ cup	red bell pepper, small dice	120 mL or 65 g
4-6	radishes, thinly sliced	4-6
4-6	green onions, thinly sliced	4-6
1 tbsp	sumac	15 mL
	salt and pepper	
	pita chips, in pieces	

1. **Make the dressing:** In a bowl, whisk the olive oil, lime juice and pomegranate molasses into an emulsion. Blend in the cinnamon and allspice. Taste and adjust the seasoning as needed. Reserve.

2. **Assemble:** In a large salad bowl, combine the parsley, mint, pomegranate seeds, tomatoes, cucumber, bell peppers, radishes and green onions. Sprinkle with sumac and season with salt and pepper.

3. **Serve:** Pour the dressing on the salad and toss well. Garnish with pita chips.

* If you can't find pomegranate molasses, put 2 cups (475 mL) of pomegranate juice and 1 tsp (5 mL) of granulated sugar in a saucepan and bring to a boil over medium-high heat. Reduce the heat to low and simmer for about 30 minutes, or until the juice has thickened into a syrup. Add a few drops of lemon juice. This will yield approximately ½ cup (120 mL) of pomegranate molasses.

SHrImP, ManGO anD AVOCaDO SaLaD

serves 4

In 30 minutes

Imagine succulent spicy sautéed shrimp matched with the tropical fruit duo of mango and avocado. I improvised this "fusion" salad for a summer picnic with friends. It's become an irresistible shared pleasure for all seasons. My in-laws Françoise and Paul like the contrast between the heat of the red pepper flakes and the cooling effect of the mangos.

	DRESSING	
¼ cup	extra-virgin olive oil	60 mL
¼ cup	freshly squeezed lime juice	60 mL
2 tbsp	white balsamic vinegar*	30 mL
1 tsp	honey, or maple syrup	5 mL
	SALAD	
16-20 or 1 lb	large shrimp, shelled and deveined	16-20 or 454 g
	salt and pepper	
pinch	red pepper flakes	pinch
1 tbsp	olive oil	15 mL
1 tbsp	unsalted butter	15 mL or 15 g
2	shallots, finely chopped	2
2	mangos, in ¾-inch (2 cm) cubes	2
2	avocados, just ripe, in ¾-inch (2 cm) cubes	2
1 cup	fresh cilantro, roughly chopped	240 mL or 30 g
¼ cup	sliced almonds, or pistachios, toasted	60 mL or 30-40 g

1. **Make the dressing:** In a bowl, whisk the olive oil, lime juice, balsamic vinegar and honey into an emulsion. Taste and adjust the seasoning as needed. Reserve.

2. **Prepare the shrimp:** Put the shrimp in a plate and pat them dry with paper towels. Season with salt and pepper and sprinkle with red pepper flakes.

3. **Cook the shallots and shrimp:** In a large frying pan, cook the shallots in the olive oil and butter over medium-low heat for 3 to 5 minutes, or until the shallots are softened. Add the shrimp and sauté over medium heat for 2 to 3 minutes per side, or until they are cooked and browned. Remove from the heat.

4. **Assemble:** In a salad bowl, combine the mangos, avocados and cilantro. Add the shallots and the shrimp.

5. **Serve:** Pour the dressing on the salad and toss. Garnish with nuts and serve.

* If you don't have white balsamic vinegar, use apple cider vinegar with a little bit of honey, as needed. Do not use red balsamic vinegar as it will darken the salad.

41

enDive, APPLe anD PancetTa Salad

In 30 minutes

serves 4

One of my favourite dishes at Lola, a brasserie on Place du Grand Sablon in Brussels, is the endive salad. Thanks to a helpful waiter there, I learned how to make endive salads that aren't bitter. It's as simple as making a dressing with walnut or hazelnut oil mixed with apple cider vinegar. My endive salads are now in great demand!

	DRESSING	
2 tbsp	apple cider vinegar	30 mL
3 tbsp	walnut or hazelnut oil	45 mL
	SALAD	
5 oz	pancetta, in ⅜-inch (1 cm) dice	142 g
4-6	medium endives, sliced	4-6
1-2	Granny Smith apples, peeled, cored and diced*	1-2
2 tbsp	freshly squeezed lemon juice	30 mL
2	radishes, finely sliced	2
2 oz	Gruyère cheese, shredded**	60 g
2 tbsp	chopped fresh parsley, curly or flat	30 mL or 4 g
2 tbsp	chopped walnuts or hazelnuts, toasted	30 mL or 20 g
	salt and pepper	2

1. **Make the dressing:** In a bowl, whisk the apple cider vinegar and the walnut, or hazelnut, oil into an emulsion. Reserve.

2. **Sauté the pancetta:** In a small frying pan, sauté the pancetta for 5 to 8 minutes over medium heat, or until it is crisp. Remove from the heat. With a perforated spoon, transfer the pancetta to a plate lined with paper towels.

3. **Assemble:** In a large salad bowl, combine the endives and the apples. Sprinkle with lemon juice to prevent them from turning brown. Add the pancetta, radishes, cheese, parsley and nuts. Mix well and season with salt and pepper.

4. **Serve:** Pour the dressing on the salad, toss well and serve.

* You can substitute other varieties of apples, such as Golden or McIntosh apples, or use pears.
** If desired, replace with other varieties of cheese, such as Emmental, Comté or Oka.

CHICKen Curry SalaD
serves 4 to 6

About 1 to 3 hours

I like recreating dishes that I've enjoyed at restaurants or fine food shops. When I lived in Toronto and craved chicken curry salad, I would go to Pusateri's Fine Foods. This is my take on their salad and since I do a lot of travelling, I can now have it anywhere and anytime.

	DRESSING	
½ cup	mayonnaise	120 mL
1 tbsp	curry powder*	15 mL or 7 g
2 tsp	freshly squeezed lemon juice	10 mL
	SALAD	
3 cups	cooked chicken breast, in ¾-inch (2 cm) cubes	700 mL or 420 g
3	celery stalks, diced	3
1	green bell pepper, seeded and diced	1
2	Granny Smith apples, peeled, cored and diced	2
½ cup	currants or raisins	120 mL or 70 g
	salt and pepper	
3	green onions, finely sliced	3
	almonds, slivered (optional)	
	mixed greens	

1. **Make the dressing:** In a small bowl, mix the mayonnaise, curry powder and lemon juice. Adjust the quantity of curry to taste**. Reserve.

2. **Assemble:** In a large salad bowl, combine the chicken, celery, green bell pepper, apples and currants or raisins. Add the dressing to the chicken mixture and toss well to coat each piece. Season with salt and pepper. Taste and adjust the quantity of mayonnaise and the seasoning as needed. Put in the refrigerator at least an hour before serving for the flavours to mingle.

3. **Serve:** Taste and adjust the seasoning. Garnish the chicken salad with the green onions and slivered almonds (optional). Serve on mixed greens.

4. **Store:** The salad will keep in the refrigerator for one day.

* *The better the quality of the curry, the stronger the taste.*
** *If desired, add 1 tsp (5 mL) of turmeric, but watch out; it stains!*

French Lentil Salad
serves 4 to 6

About 1 to 3 hours

Among the many wonderful dishes served at Toronto's Patachou Café, which sadly closed its doors in 2014, was the lentil salad made with Puy lentils. These small French lentils are unique because they keep their shape during cooking, and that means they give extra texture and crunch to a salad. This is my version of their salad and it's delicious with fish or meat, or simply served as a dish on its own. Oh, so French!

	LENTILS	
1 cup	Puy lentils, rinsed and drained	240 mL or 190 g
	VEGETABLES	
1 tbsp	unsalted butter	15 mL or 15 g
1-2	shallots, finely chopped	1-2
3-4	celery stalks, diced	3-4
3-4	green onions, sliced	3-4
1 cup or 4 oz	white mushrooms, sliced (optional)	240 mL or 115 g
	sea salt and pepper	
	DRESSING AND GARNISH	
2 tbsp	extra-virgin olive oil	30 mL
3 tbsp	red wine vinegar	45 mL
2 tbsp	freshly squeezed lemon juice	30 mL
10-12	sundried tomatoes, in oil or not, chopped	10-12
¼ cup	sunflower seeds	60 mL or 35 g
	extra-virgin olive oil	
¼ cup	fresh basil leaves, in thin ribbons	60 mL or 15 g

1. **Cook the lentils:** In a saucepan, cook the lentils uncovered in salted boiling water according to the package instructions, or until the lentils are al dente. Drain and set aside.

2. **Cook the vegetables:** In a frying pan, cook the shallots, celery, green onions and mushrooms (optional) in the butter over medium-low heat for 4 to 6 minutes, or until the vegetables are lightly browned and still a bit crunchy. Season with salt and pepper. Remove from the heat and reserve.

3. **Assemble:** In a salad bowl, combine the lentils and the cooked vegetables. Sprinkle with olive oil, red wine vinegar and lemon juice. The warm lentils and vegetables will absorb the flavours of the dressing. Add the sundried tomatoes and sunflower seeds. Toss well, taste and adjust the seasoning as needed. Put in the refrigerator at least one hour before serving for the flavours to mingle.

4. **Serve:** Taste and adjust the seasoning. Drizzle with olive oil and garnish with the basil ribbons.

5. **Store:** The lentil salad will keep in the refrigerator for 2 to 3 days.

caesar salad
serves 6 to 8

Less than one hour

This is the Food Network's recipe and happily, it's true to the first Caesar salad created in 1924 by Caesar Cardini, an Italian chef living in San Diego. The dressing is lighter than the one used in most Caesar salads. It's the tangy spicy taste of the dressing that appeals to my in-laws Colette and Pierre. As for me, I'm hooked on the croutons. See how long you can hold out before you dig into the salad!

	CROUTONS	
1 tbsp	anchovy paste, or 4-5 anchovy fillets, puréed	15 mL or 10 g
½ cup	extra-virgin olive oil	120 mL
1 tsp	freshly cracked black peppercorns	5 mL or 3 g
1	loaf of bread, with crust, in 1-inch (2.5 cm) cubes	1
	DRESSING	
1	large egg, at refrigerator temperature	1
3 tbsp	red wine vinegar	45 mL
2 tbsp	freshly squeezed lemon juice	30 mL
1 tbsp	puréed garlic	15 mL
2 tsp	dry mustard	10 mL or 6 g
1 tsp	celery salt	5 mL or 5 g
3 dashes	Tabasco sauce	3 dashes
3 dashes	Worcestershire sauce	3 dashes
	SALAD	
2	heads of romaine lettuce, torn in pieces	2
½ cup	shaved Parmesan cheese	120 mL or 60 g

1. **Prepare the anchovy mixture:** In a small food processor, combine the anchovy paste, olive oil and black peppercorns. Purée until the mixture is smooth. Reserve.

2. **Make the croutons*:** In a large bowl, combine the bread cubes with ⅓ cup (80 mL) of the reserved anchovy mixture. Mix well to coat each cube. In a large frying pan, sauté the bread cubes over medium heat for 10 to 15 minutes, or until the cubes are browned and crisp. Remove from the heat and reserve.

3. **Cook the egg:** In a small saucepan, cook the egg in boiling water for exactly 1½ minutes. Remove from the water and reserve. The egg will be barely cooked.

4. **Make the dressing:** In the bottom of a large salad bowl, combine the remaining anchovy mixture, red wine vinegar, lemon juice, garlic, dry mustard, celery salt, Tabasco, Worcestershire sauce and the shelled egg. Whisk until the dressing is emulsified. Taste and adjust the seasoning as needed.

5. **Assemble and serve:** Add the torn lettuce pieces, croutons and Parmesan to the dressing. Toss well and serve.

* The croutons can be prepared in advance. To make sure that the croutons are crisp when ready to serve, give them a quick toss in a frying pan, or quickly crisp them up in the oven.

49

TABBOULEH WITH QUINOA
serves 4

About 1 to 3 hours

Recently, I decided to update my recipe by using protein-rich quinoa instead of bulgur. All the other ingredients of this classic Lebanese dish are there — parsley, mint, onion, tomatoes, garlic and lemon juice. Ideal as a side dish, this tabbouleh is simple to prepare and very healthy. No reason to hold back, is there?

½ cup	quinoa	120 mL or 90 g
2 cups	fresh curly parsley	475 mL or 60 g
½ cup	fresh mint leaves	120 mL or 15 g
¼ cup	finely chopped onion	60 mL or 35 g
12-15	cherry tomatoes, cut in half	12-15
1	garlic clove, minced	1
¼ cup	freshly squeezed lemon juice	60 mL
	salt and pepper	
2 tbsp	extra-virgin olive oil	30 mL
1	lemon, in wedges	1

1. **Cook the quinoa:** In a saucepan, cook the quinoa covered in salted boiling water according to the package instructions, or until it is al dente. Drain and set aside.

2. **Chop the herbs:** In a food processor, finely chop the parsley and the mint leaves.

3. **Assemble:** In a salad bowl, combine the quinoa, parsley, mint, onion, tomatoes and garlic. Sprinkle with lemon juice. Season with salt and pepper and toss well. Put in the refrigerator for at least an hour before serving for the flavours to mingle.

4. **Serve:** Taste and adjust the seasoning. Drizzle with the olive oil and serve with the lemon wedges. The tabbouleh is equally delicious cold or at room temperature.

vegetables
anything but boring — from side dish to centre stage

roasted cauliflower and fennel
serves 4

Less than one hour

I was inspired by a starter served at Cucina Enoteca, a restaurant in Del Mar, California where my husband and I would often go with our friends Bonni and Bob. It's surprising how tasty roasted cauliflower is compared to the plain-Jane steamed version. As the cauliflower and fennel roast together, they become caramelized and slightly charred. The dish is served on a tahini-yogourt sauce with an unusual garnish of currants, pine nuts and fresh dill. After testing the recipe in their own homes, our friends Carol and Tony, Lindsay and John, Marie and Paul, all agreed that it's finger-lickin' good.

	VEGETABLES	
1	medium cauliflower	1
1	fennel	1
¼ cup	extra-virgin olive oil	60 mL
	sea salt and pepper	
	SAUCE	
¼ cup	tahini	60 mL
¼ cup	plain Greek yogourt	60 mL
1	garlic clove, minced	1
1 tbsp	freshly squeezed lemon juice	15 mL
1 tsp	maple syrup, or honey	5 mL
	GARNISH	
	currants	
¼ cup	pine nuts, toasted	60 mL or 40 g
	fresh dill, chopped	

1. **Prepare the oven:** Place the oven rack in the top position and preheat the oven to 425 °F (220 °C).

2. **Prepare the vegetables:** On a cutting board, cut the cauliflower in florets and the fennel in strips. Put them in a large bowl. Pour in the olive oil and toss well to coat. Add more olive oil, if needed. Season with salt and pepper.

3. Place the vegetables in a single layer on a sheet pan without crowding them. Use a second sheet pan if needed.

4. **Bake** in the oven for 20 to 25 minutes, or until the vegetables are caramelized. If desired, set the oven to broil and continue cooking for a few minutes. Remove from the oven and reserve. Repeat with the second sheet pan, if necessary.

5. **Make the sauce:** Blend the tahini, yogourt, garlic, lemon juice and maple syrup, or honey, in a food processor until the sauce is creamy. If the sauce is too thick, add a bit of warm water.

6. **Serve:** Spread the tahini-yogourt sauce on the bottom of a warmed serving plate, set the vegetables on top and garnish with the currants, pine nuts, and fresh dill. Serve warm.

7. **Store:** This dish can be prepared in advance and will keep in the refrigerator for 1 to 2 days. Warm up in the oven before serving.

seasoned sweet potato fries
serves 4

Less than one hour

Grazing on these fries is like indulging in real French fries without the guilt because they're baked, not deep-fried. The sweet potato fries served at the small organic restaurant God Save the Cream in Brussels motivated me to make them at home with my own seasoning blend. I came up with a three-spice combo of cumin, fennel and mustard that filled my kitchen with the seductive fragrance of Indian cuisine.

2-3 or 1½-2 lb	large sweet potatoes, peeled*	2-3 or 675-900 g
¼ cup	extra-virgin olive oil	60 mL
1 tbsp	blend of ground cumin, fennel and mustard seeds, in equal quantities**	15 mL
pinch	sea salt	pinch

1. **Prepare the oven:** Place the oven rack in the top position and preheat the oven to 425 °F (220 °C).

2. **Prepare the sweet potatoes:** On a cutting board, cut the sweet potatoes in ½-inch (1.25 cm) sticks and place them in a large bowl. Pour in the olive oil and toss well to coat. Add more olive oil, if needed. Sprinkle the spice blend evenly over the potatoes and mix well so that each stick is lightly seasoned. Add salt and pepper.

3. Place the sweet potatoes sticks in a single layer on a sheet pan without crowding them. Use a second sheet pan if needed.

4. **Bake** in the oven for 20 to 25 minutes, or until the sweet potatoes are browned. If desired, set the oven to broil and continue baking for a few more minutes. Remove from the oven and reserve. Repeat with the second sheet pan, if necessary.

5. **Serve** hot, with a pinch of sea salt***.

*   Selected grocery stores sell sweet potatoes pre-cut into sticks.
**   This dish can be prepared with a variety of seasonings; your turn to play with flavours!
*** The sweet potato fries are best when they are fresh out of the oven.

ZUCCHINI BLINIS
makes 6 to 8 blinis

About 1 to 3 hours

I'm always on the lookout for dishes that can both impress my guests and be made in advance. The September 2013 edition of House and Home *magazine had a zucchini pancake recipe that fit the bill. I eliminated an egg, added pine nuts, and renamed the pancakes as blinis. You can serve them with plain yogourt or sour cream as an appetizer, or as a side dish with meat or fish. They would even make great sliders.*

	ZUCCHINI	
2-3 or 1½ lb	medium zucchini, unpeeled	2-3 or 675 g
1 tsp	salt	5 mL
	MIXTURE	
2 tbsp	olive oil	30 mL
2 tbsp	unsalted butter	30 mL
1	medium onion, finely chopped	1
2	large eggs, lightly beaten	2
7 oz	feta cheese, crumbled	200 g
¼ cup	chopped fresh flat parsley	60 mL or 8 g
¼ cup	chopped fresh dill fronds	60 mL or 8 g
¼ cup	pine nuts, toasted	60 mL or 40 g
⅓ cup	all-purpose flour	80 mL or 40 g
	salt and pepper	
	TOPPING	
	plain yogourt or sour cream	
	fresh dill fronds, chopped	

1. **Prepare the oven and sheet pan:** Place the oven rack in the middle position and preheat the oven to 350 °F (180 °C). Line a sheet pan with parchment paper.

2. **Prepare the zucchini:** Grate the zucchini using the large holes of a box grater and transfer to a colander. Salt and let drain for 30 minutes. Press to squeeze the excess water, put in a plate and pat dry with paper towels. This step is important to prevent the mixture in step 4 from being too liquid.

3. **Cook the onion:** In a large non-stick frying pan, cook the onion in 1 tbsp (15 mL) of the olive oil and 1 tbsp (15 mL) of the butter over medium heat for 4 to 5 minutes, or until the onion is softened. Reserve.

4. **Combine the mixture:** In a large bowl, mix the grated zucchini, onion, eggs, feta cheese, parsley, dill and pine nuts. With a spatula, incorporate the flour until just blended in. Season with pepper to taste, and salt sparingly as feta is already salty.

5. **Cook the blinis:** In the same frying pan, heat the remaining 1 tbsp (15 mL) of olive oil and 1 tbsp (15 mL) of butter over medium-high heat. Working in two batches, drop in several dollops of ¼ cup (60 mL) of the zucchini mixture to make blinis about 3 inches (7.5 cm) in diameter, making sure to space them in the pan. Cook the blinis for 4 to 5 minutes per side before turning them, or until they are nicely browned. As the blinis are ready, place them on the sheet pan. You should have 6 to 8 blinis. Continue to cook the blinis in the oven for 8 to 10 minutes. Reserve.

6. **Serve:** Put the blinis on a serving plate, garnish with plain yogourt or sour cream, and sprinkle with dill. The blinis can be made 1 or 2 days in advance and stored in the refrigerator. Reheat in the oven before serving.

RaTaTOUILLe
serves 8 to 10

I discovered this classic Provençal dish 40 years ago when my cousin Rachel and I were vacationing in Nice and we were determined to eat local specialties. Since then, I've tested various versions of this slowly cooked vegetable stew and, for me, it really shines when the vegetables hold their shape, colour, and especially flavour. The key to success: don't cut the vegetables too small and don't cook the stew for too long.

2	medium onions	2
1 of each	bell peppers: green, red and yellow	1 of each
2-3	medium zucchini, unpeeled	2-3
1	medium eggplant, unpeeled	1
4	medium tomatoes, peeled and seeded	4
5 tbsp	olive oil	75 mL
2	garlic cloves, minced	2
	salt and pepper	
2 tbsp	tomato paste	30 mL
1	bouquet garni*, or 1 tsp of herbes de Provence	1
¼ cup	freshly squeezed lemon juice	60 mL
6-8	basil leaves, in thin ribbons	6-8

1. **Cut the vegetables:** On a cutting board, cut the onions, bell peppers, zucchini, eggplant and tomatoes into 1-inch (2.5 cm) cubes. Set the tomatoes aside.

2. **Sauté the onions and bell peppers:** In a Dutch oven, sauté the onions and the bell peppers in 2 tbsp (30 mL) of the olive oil over medium-low heat for 8 to 10 minutes, or until the onions and bell peppers are browned. Add the garlic and season with salt and pepper. Turn off the heat and reserve.

3. **Sauté the zucchini:** In a frying pan, sauté the zucchini cubes in 1 tbsp (15 mL) of the olive oil over medium heat for 10 to 12 minutes, or until the cubes are browned. Season with salt and pepper and put in the Dutch oven with the onions and bell peppers.

4. **Sauté the eggplant:** Using the same frying pan, sauté the eggplant cubes in 2 tbsp (30 mL) of the olive oil over medium heat for 10-12 minutes, or until the cubes are browned. Add more olive oil as needed. Season with salt and pepper and put in the Dutch oven with the other vegetables.

5. **Assemble and cook the ratatouille:** Add the tomatoes, tomato paste, bouquet garni, or herbes de Provence, and lemon juice to the Dutch oven. Stir. Cover and simmer over low heat for 30 minutes, stirring from time to time. Uncover and continue cooking over low heat for 30 minutes, or until the vegetables have softened and still have colour. Remove from the heat and reserve.

6. **Serve:** Taste and adjust the seasoning. Serve hot, at room temperature or cold, with a drizzle of olive oil and ribbons of basil. Ratatouille is also delicious with a topping of grated Parmesan cheese or crumbled feta cheese.

7. **Store:** Ratatouille will keep in the refrigerator for about 3 days.

---

* *Bouquet garni is the name for a bundle of fresh herbs, usually thyme, parsley and bay leaf, tied together in a "bouquet". It is also available dried in a jar or in a sachet at grocery stores.*

Spinach Italian-Style
serves 6 to 8

About 1 to 3 hours

I've been making this savoury dish for many years. It's like a quiche without a crust — just spinach with béchamel sauce and Parmesan. I made a few changes* to Margo Oliver's recipe called "Épinards à l'italienne" in her 1972 book Perspectives — Les Menus. *As a food editor and cookbook writer, Margo Oliver influenced Canadian cuisine for many decades.*

	SPINACH	
3 x 10 oz	bags of fresh spinach**	3 x 285 g
	BÉCHAMEL SAUCE	
¼ cup	unsalted butter	60 mL or 56 g
¼ cup	all-purpose flour	60 mL or 30 g
½ tsp	salt	2.5 mL
¼ tsp	pepper	1 mL
1 cup	milk, 2% or whole, at room temperature	240 mL
2	large eggs	2
1 cup	grated Parmesan cheese	240 mL or 90 g
pinch	nutmeg, ground or freshly grated	pinch

1. **Prepare the oven and baking dish:** Place the oven rack in the middle position and preheat the oven to 375 °F (190 °C). Butter a 4-cup (1 L) baking dish.

2. **Cook and chop the spinach:** In a stockpot, put the spinach in about 1 inch (2.5 cm) of water. Cover and bring to a boil. Reduce the heat and continue to cook covered for 5 to 6 minutes, or until the spinach is cooked. Drain well in a colander by pressing firmly to remove all the excess water. Transfer to a cutting board and chop finely. Reserve.

3. **Make the béchamel sauce:** In a saucepan, melt the butter over medium heat. Add the flour and stir with a whisk until it starts bubbling. Season with salt and pepper. Add the milk all at once while stirring with a whisk. Continue to cook over medium heat and stir for 3 to 5 minutes, or until the sauce starts to bubble and is smooth and thick.

4. **Assemble:** Add the spinach to the sauce and cook over low heat for 3 minutes while stirring. Remove from the heat and let rest for 3 minutes. Add the eggs, ¾ cup (180 mL) of the Parmesan cheese and nutmeg. Put it back over low heat and mix with a wooden spoon until the sauce is smooth. Remove from the heat. Pour the spinach mixture into the baking dish and sprinkle with the remaining Parmesan cheese.

5. **Bake** in the oven for 50 to 60 minutes, or until the top of the spinach is nicely browned.

6. **Serve:** Let cool for 5 to 10 minutes before serving. This dish is ideal to serve with the Chicken Marengo (page 93).

7. **Store:** This spinach dish will keep in the refrigerator for 3 to 4 days or in the freezer for 2 to 3 months

* Margo Oliver's recipe added an egg yolk and used half as much Parmesan cheese.
** The fresh spinach can be replaced by 2 x 10 oz (285 g) packages of frozen spinach.

pasta and rice
comfort food for young and old

mac 'n' cheese
serves 6 to 8

Less than one hour

Who didn't grow up on mac 'n' cheese? This guilty pleasure brings back many happy childhood memories. If you're looking for a sophisticated version made with prosciutto, goat cheese, truffle oil or the like, this recipe is not for you. I'm perfectly content to stick to classic comfort food that I brighten up with a topping of sliced tomatoes. Philip, my son, gives this dish his unbiased seal of approval.

	PASTA	
8 oz	macaroni	225 g
	CHEESE SAUCE	
¼ cup	unsalted butter	60 mL or 56 g
¼ cup	all-purpose flour	60 mL or 30 g
1 tsp	dry mustard	5 mL or 3 g
¼ tsp	nutmeg, ground or freshly grated	1 mL
2 cups	milk, 2% or whole, at room temperature	475 mL
	salt and pepper	
6 oz	Cheddar cheese, medium or strong, shredded	170 g
4 oz	Gruyère cheese, shredded	115 g
	TOPPING	
2-3	medium tomatoes, sliced*	2-3
	breadcrumbs	
	Parmesan cheese, grated	

1. **Prepare the oven:** Place the oven rack in the middle position and preheat the oven to 375 °F (190 °C).

2. **Cook the macaroni:** In a large saucepan, cook the macaroni in salted boiling water according to the package instructions, or until the pasta is al dente. Drain and set aside in a colander.

3. **Make the sauce:** In the same saucepan, melt the butter over medium heat. Add the flour, dry mustard and nutmeg and cook while stirring with a whisk for about 2 minutes. Pour in the warm milk slowly and whisk until the mixture just starts to bubble. Reduce the heat to medium-low and stir until the sauce is smooth and thick, or about 1 to 2 minutes. Remove from the heat. Add the cheeses and stir to melt.

4. **Assemble:** Add the macaroni to the cheese sauce and mix with a wooden spoon over medium-low heat until the macaroni is coated. Transfer to an 8-by-12-inch (20 cm by 30 cm) baking dish. Garnish the macaroni with the sliced tomatoes and sprinkle with the breadcrumbs and Parmesan cheese.

5. **Bake** in the oven for 20-25 minutes, or until the cheese sauce starts to bubble around the edges. If the topping needs more browning, set the oven to broil and cook for a few minutes. Do not overbake to ensure that the sauce stays creamy.

6. **Serve:** Let cool for 10 minutes before serving.

* *Medium tomatoes can be replaced by cherry tomatoes cut in half.*

Mamie's Bolognese sauce
serves 8 to 10

About 1 to 3 hours

Also called "la sauce de spaghetti de Mamie" by her grandchildren, this Bolognese sauce is one of my mother's signature dishes and one that she continues to make often. When my sisters, my brothers and I were still living at home and my mother would serve spaghetti with Bolognese sauce, my father would rub his hands together and exclaim "Allora" in anticipation of a hearty, heart-warming meal with a glass of good red wine.

	MEAT	
1½ lb	mix of ground beef, pork, and veal*	675 g
4 tbsp	olive oil	60 mL
	salt and pepper	
	VEGETABLES AND SAUCE	
1	medium onion	1
2-3	celery stalks	2-3
1	green pepper	1
1	medium carrot	1
2-3	garlic cloves, minced	2-3
1	bay leaf	1
1 cup	dry red wine	240 mL
1 can of 14 oz	diced tomatoes	1 can of 398 mL
2 cans of 28 oz	seasoned tomato sauce**	2 cans of 796 mL
pinch of each	dried oregano and dried thyme	pinch of each
pinch	red pepper flakes	pinch
	GARNISH	
	Parmesan cheese, shaved	
	fresh flat parsley, chopped	

1. **Brown the meat:** In a heavy-bottomed frying pan, brown the meat in 2 tbsp (30 mL) of the olive oil over medium-high heat, by crumbling it with a wooden spoon. Season with salt and pepper. Cook until the meat has lost its pink colour and is browned. Reserve.

2. **Cut and soften the vegetables:** On a cutting board, cut the onion, celery, bell pepper and carrot in ½-inch (1.25 cm) dice. Put the vegetables in a Dutch oven and soften them in 2 tbsp (30 mL) of the olive oil over medium-low heat for 5 to 8 minutes.

3. **Assemble:** Add the cooked meat and its juices to the Dutch oven. Add the garlic and bay leaf. Pour in the red wine and simmer over medium heat for 5 to 8 minutes. Add the diced tomatoes with their juice and the tomato sauce. Season with oregano, thyme, red pepper flakes, salt and pepper, to taste.

4. **Simmer the sauce:** Stir and bring to a boil over medium-high heat. Reduce the heat to low, cover partially and simmer for at least 60 minutes to allow the sauce to thicken. Stir frequently to prevent the sauce from burning on the bottom. Remove the bay leaf. Remove from the heat and let cool.

5. **Serve:** Heat and serve with pasta al dente, topped with shaved Parmesan cheese and parsley. In Italy, sauces are paired with specific pasta shapes. For a meat sauce like Bolognese to cling to pasta, Italians would match it with large shells (conchiglie), tubes (ziti, rigatoni, penne), or long wide and flat pasta (tagliatelle and pappardelle).

6. **Store:** The sauce will keep in the refrigerator for 3 to 5 days or in the freezer for 2 to 3 months.

* *Buy the mix of ground beef, pork, and veal prepackaged at the grocery store, or combine ½ lb (225 g) of each of the ground meats.*

** *I use Hunt's Italian tomato sauce and Classico's sundried tomato sauce, together.*

Bolognese Lasagna
serves 6 to 8

About 1 to 3 hours

There's nothing like piping hot lasagna to draw a crowd to the table. And it certainly gets my sister Elise's attention! When our kids were school age, we would go away for March break with our friends and their family. We would take turns making meals, and my first contribution was always my mother's lasagna because it can be made in advance and heated up when needed. I'd add a green salad, everyone would dig in and our week away would be off to a great start.

3 cups or 30 oz	ricotta cheese	700 mL or 850 g
2	large eggs, beaten	2
1 tsp	salt	5 mL
½ tsp	pepper	2.5 mL
¼ cup	chopped fresh parsley, curly or flat	60 mL or 8 g
½ cup	grated Parmesan cheese	120 mL or 45 g
1 lb	mozzarella cheese, sliced	454 g
4-5 cups	Mamie's Bolognese Sauce (page 69)*	950 mL - 1.2 L
9-12	lasagna noodles, oven-ready	9-12
2 oz	goat cheese (optional)	60 g

1. **Prepare the oven and baking dish:** Place the oven rack in the middle position and preheat the oven to 375 °F (190 °C). Lightly butter an 8-by-12-inch (20 cm by 30 cm) baking dish.

2. **Make the filling:** In a large bowl, combine the ricotta, eggs, salt, pepper, parsley and Parmesan cheese. Mix with a wooden spoon until the filling is smooth.

3. **Assemble:** Place 3 or 4 lasagna noodles on the bottom of the baking dish. Spread ⅓ of the ricotta filling. Layer ¼ of the mozzarella slices and cover with ⅓ of the Bolognese sauce. Repeat for two more layers and finish with the last ¼ of mozzarella slices. Optional: For a sophisticated touch in your lasagna, add nuggets of goat cheese on top of each layer of the ricotta filling.

4. **Bake and serve:** Cover the baking dish with aluminum foil and bake in the oven for 30 to 40 minutes, or until the lasagna is bubbly. At half-time, remove the foil to brown the top of the lasagna. Remove from the oven and let rest for 10 minutes before serving.

5. **Store:** The lasagna will keep in the refrigerator for 3 to 5 days or in the freezer for 2 to 3 months.

* Or use homemade or commercially available meat-and-tomato sauce.

NOODLES WITH CHICKEN and PEANUT SAUCE

serves 4 to 6

Less than one hour

Children adore pasta. Punch it up with chicken and peanut sauce, and they will be over the moon. And their parents too! If you do the prep work in advance*, dinner can be served in under 30 minutes. This dish has always been my son Philip's favourite. In fact, it's been #1 on his top five, from the time he was a teenager up to now as a professional in Toronto. He still insists on having it every time he's back home for a visit.

	CHICKEN	
3-4 or 1½-2 lb	chicken breasts, boneless, skinless	3-4 or 675-900 g
2 tbsp	olive oil	30 mL
	PEANUT SAUCE	
½ cup	natural peanut butter, unsweetened	120 mL
½ cup	soya sauce	120 mL
½ cup	maple syrup	120 mL
1 tsp	rice vinegar	5 mL
1 tsp	sesame oil	5 mL
	NOODLES	
16 oz	spaghetti, linguine, or Asian rice vermicelli	454 g
2 cups	carrots, in matchsticks	475 mL or 190 g
	TOPPING	
3-4	green onions, sliced	3-4
	peanuts or cashews, chopped	
	cilantro leaves, chopped	
1	lime, in wedges	1

1. **Prepare the oven:** Place the oven rack in the middle position and preheat the oven to 400 °F (200 °C).

2. **Cook the chicken:** Coat the chicken breasts with olive oil and season with salt and pepper. Put the chicken on a sheet pan and cook in the oven for 20 minutes, or until the chicken is no longer pink inside (165 °F or 74 °C). Let cool before shredding the chicken into bite-size pieces with your fingers. Keep warm under a sheet of aluminum foil.

3. **Make the sauce:** In a food processor or a blender, combine the peanut butter, soya sauce, maple syrup, rice vinegar and sesame oil and blend until the sauce is smooth. Pour into a small saucepan and warm up over low heat. Keep warm.

4. **Cook the pasta and carrots:** In a large saucepan, cook the pasta in salted boiling water according to the package instructions. Approximately 2 to 3 minutes before the indicated cooking time, toss in the carrot matchsticks. Cook until the pasta and the carrots are al dente. Drain and put back in the saucepan.

5. **Assemble and serve:** Add the chicken pieces to the pasta and carrots, pour in half of the warm peanut sauce and toss. The sauce will be absorbed by the warm pasta. Transfer to a warmed serving dish. Garnish with the green onions, peanuts or cashews, and cilantro. Serve immediately with the rest of the peanut sauce and the lime quarters on the side. This dish is delicious with broccoli florets or, for an Asian touch, with edamame.

* The chicken and peanut sauce can be prepared in advance (steps 1 to 3) and refrigerated for 3 to 4 days.

Pasta with Shrimp, Tomatoes and Feta

serves 4

In 30 minutes

Necessity is the mother of invention. It was a magical summer afternoon that turned into an evening and our friends lingered on longer than expected. Suddenly, I had to put together a meal with whatever was on hand. If you like delicious unpredictability, you will enjoy this dish. How large are the shrimp? How juicy are the tomatoes? How creamy is the feta? In the end, it doesn't matter. It always comes out just right, as it did for Marie and Don, Caroline and Marc, Nathalie and Caroline . . .

	SHRIMP	
2 tbsp	olive oil	30 mL
2 tbsp	unsalted butter	30 mL or 30 g
16-20 or 1 lb	large shrimp, shelled and deveined	16-20 or 454 g
	salt and pepper	
pinch	red pepper flakes	pinch
	TOMATO AND FETA SAUCE	
1	medium onion, chopped	1
2	garlic cloves, minced	2
12 oz	cherry tomatoes, cut in half*	340 g
8 oz	feta cheese, diced	225 g
¼ cup	dry white wine	60 mL
1 tbsp	freshly squeezed lemon juice	15 mL
	salt and pepper	
	PASTA	
16 oz	spaghetti, linguine or tagliatelle	454 g
	TOPPING	
¼ cup	pine nuts, toasted	60 mL or 40 g
¼ cup	chopped fresh parsley, curly or flat	60 mL or 8 g

1. Sauté the shrimp: In a large frying pan, sauté the shrimp in 1 tbsp (15 mL) of the olive oil and 1 tbsp (15 mL) of the butter over medium heat for 2 to 3 minutes per side, or until they are cooked and browned. Season with salt, pepper and red pepper flakes. Put aside and keep warm.

2. Make the sauce: In the same frying pan, soften the onion in 1 tbsp (15 mL) of the olive oil and 1 tbsp (15 mL) of the butter over medium-low heat for 3 to 5 minutes. Add the garlic and stir. Add the tomatoes and feta cheese. Stir gently and cook for 3 to 5 minutes. Add the white wine and simmer uncovered over low heat for 8 to 10 minutes, or until the tomatoes start to soften and the feta cheese starts to melt. If the sauce is not juicy enough, add a bit more of the white wine.

3. Cook the pasta: Meanwhile, in a large saucepan, cook the pasta in salted boiling water according to the package instructions, or until the pasta is al dente. Drain and reserve.

4. Assemble: Add the shrimp to the sauce and reheat for a few minutes. Season with the lemon juice, salt and pepper. Keep warm.

5. Serve: Divide the pasta on warmed plates and spoon the shrimp in the tomato-feta sauce over the pasta. Garnish with pine nuts and parsley. Serve immediately.

* Other types of tomatoes, cut in pieces, can replace the cherry tomatoes.

MUSHROOM RISOTTO
serves 4

Less than one hour

Risotto — what a musical word for a rich and comforting dish of creamy grains of rice! I almost never order it in restaurants because I am convinced that it can never be as good as the one my mother makes. Only recently, I discovered that my son-in-law David's risotto is just as delicious as hers. We really need to compare recipes.

2 cups	chicken broth*	475 mL
2 cups or 8 oz	sliced white mushrooms**	475 mL or 225 g
6 tbsp	unsalted butter, divided	90 mL or 85 g
1	medium onion, finely chopped	1
1 cup	arborio rice***	240 mL or 190 g
1 cup	dry white wine	240 mL
½ cup	grated Parmesan cheese, divided	120 ml or 60 g
	salt and pepper	
	fresh flat parsley, chopped	

1. **Warm the chicken broth** in a small saucepan over low heat and keep warm.

2. **Sauté the mushrooms** in a small frying pan in 2 tbsp (30 mL) of the butter over medium-low heat for 5 to 8 minutes, or until they are browned. Reserve.

3. **Cook the onion** in a large frying pan in 2 tbsp (30 mL) of the butter over medium heat for 4 to 5 minutes, or until the onion is softened.

4. **Make the risotto:** Add the arborio rice and stir with a wooden spoon over medium heat for 1 to 2 minutes to coat the rice with butter, without letting it brown. Add the white wine and stir constantly for 2 to 3 minutes, or until the wine is completely absorbed. Add a ladle of the warm broth and continue stirring until the broth is absorbed. Repeat with the rest of the broth, while stirring, one ladle at a time every 3 to 4 minutes, or until the broth is absorbed. This step should take approximately 20 to 25 minutes. The rice should be al dente and very creamy. Remove from the heat.

5. Add half of the Parmesan cheese and the rest of the butter. Mix until both are melted. Taste and season with salt and pepper as needed. Add the mushrooms and stir.

6. Serve immediately in warmed bowls. Sprinkle with the rest of the Parmesan cheese and parsley.

*   For a vegetarian version of the risotto, use vegetable broth.
**   Try the risotto with other mushroom varieties, green peas or fresh asparagus tips.
*** Arborio rice, a variety from northern Italy, is a short-grain rice with a creamy texture. This type of rice is essential to make authentic risotto.

sautéed and grilled

SIMPLE, FAST, AND WITH A TWIST

veal scallops
with yogourt sauce
serves 4

Less than one hour

Because they're cut very thin, veal scallops cook up in a flash. They wait for no one so everything else must be in place when the scallops are done — the table set, side dishes prepped, wine uncorked, serving dishes and dinner plates warmed up. Your guests will be eager to enjoy the ever-so-tender veal in a sauce that they'll swear is made with cream.

	VEAL	
1½-2 lb	veal scallops*	675-900 g
2 tbsp	olive oil	30 mL
	salt and pepper	
	YOGOURT SAUCE	
1 cup	5% plain Greek yogourt**	240 mL
	GARNISH	
	fresh parsley, curly or flat, chopped	
1	lemon, in wedges	1

1. **Prepare the veal:** Put the veal scallops on a plate and pat them dry with paper towels. Baste them with the olive oil. Season with salt and pepper, to taste. Cover and let rest at room temperature for 30 minutes.

2. **Cook the veal:** In a very hot cast iron frying pan, without overcrowding the pan, sear the scallops undisturbed for about 1 minute per side, or until the meat is lightly browned. Do not overcook! Transfer the scallops to a warmed serving dish and loosely cover with aluminum foil. Adjust the heat if needed and repeat with the remaining scallops. Reserve.

3. **Make the sauce:** Reduce the heat to low, add the yogourt to the frying pan and use a wooden spoon to scrape the brown bits and deglaze the pan. After a few minutes of stirring, the yogourt will become a smooth, creamy and pale brown sauce.

4. **Serve:** Pour the sauce over the scallops and garnish with parsley. Serve immediately with the lemon wedges on warmed plates. As a side dish, serve Zucchini Blinis (page 59) or Ratatouille (page 61).

* *Allow approximately 6-8 oz (170-225 g) of veal scallops per person.*
** *If the yogourt is too light (0% or 2%), it will separate, and the sauce will be runny instead of creamy.*

FILET MIGNON
WITH RED WINE AND SOYA SAUCE
serves 4

Less than one hour

I grew up in a family of five children at a time when Sunday dinners usually meant that roast beef was on the menu. Times have changed, and even if I now eat less red meat, I still like to indulge in a good steak once in a while. For these special occasions, I treat myself to pan-seared filet mignon in a sauce packed with unforgettable umami flavour. When you serve it to your meat-loving guests, they won't stop talking about it for days!

	MEAT	
4 or 1½-2 lb	filets mignons*	4 or 675–900 g
2 tbsp	olive oil	30 mL
	black pepper	
	RED WINE AND SOYA SAUCE	
½ cup	dry red wine	120 mL
½ cup	soya sauce	120 mL
¼ cup	Dijon mustard	60 mL
¼ cup	tomato juice	60 mL

1. **Prepare the oven:** Place the oven rack in the middle position and preheat the oven to 400 °F (200 °C).

2. **Prepare the meat:** Put the filets mignons on a plate and pat them dry with paper towels. Baste them with olive oil and season with pepper, to taste. Salting is not necessary because of the salt in the soya sauce. Cover and let rest at room temperature for 30 minutes.

3. **Make the sauce:** In a bowl, mix the red wine, soya sauce, Dijon mustard and tomato juice and whisk until the sauce is smooth. Reserve.

4. **Sear the meat:** In a very hot cast iron frying pan, sear the filets undisturbed for 2 to 3 minutes per side, or until the meat is nicely browned. Transfer the meat to an ovenproof dish and pour the sauce around the filets.

5. **Cook the meat** in the oven for approximately 10 to 12 minutes, or until the meat is almost medium-rare (140 °F or 60 °C). The cooking time will depend on the thickness of the meat and the desired doneness.

6. **Rest the meat and serve:** Remove from the oven, lightly cover with aluminum foil and let rest for 8 to 10 minutes for the juices to settle into the meat. The meat will continue to cook as it rests. When ready to serve, coat each filet mignon with the sauce.

* Allow one filet of approximately 6-8 oz (170-225 g) per person.

saLMon MonTReaL-STYLe

Less than one hour

Whenever I visit Toronto, my friend Catherine insists on inviting me over for a meal. And one of those times she served a salmon dish. After just one bite, I had to know what made the salmon taste so special. With a twinkle in her eye, she revealed her secret: Montreal Steak Spice. Yes, using a steak spice brings salmon to a whole new level.

	FISH	
4 or 1½-2 lb	salmon, centre cut fillets, skin-on*	4 or 675-900 g
4 tsp	Montreal Steak Spice**	20 mL or 24 g
2 tsp	olive oil	10 mL
	GARNISH	
	fresh dill fronds	
1	lemon, in wedges	1

1. **Prepare the salmon:** Put the salmon fillets on a plate and pat them dry with paper towels. Place the flesh side up and sprinkle it with Montreal Steak Spice. Cover and let rest at room temperature for 30 minutes.

2. **Cook the salmon:** Heat the oil in a large non-stick frying pan over medium-high heat. Place the salmon fillets skin-side down and cook over medium heat for 6 to 8 minutes without turning them. As the fish cooks, the salmon skin will render a little fat into the frying pan. Adjust the heat as needed. Using a fish spatula, turn the fillets over and continue cooking for 5 to 6 minutes, or until the salmon is browned on the outside and slightly undercooked on the inside (120 °F or 49 °C).

3. **Rest the salmon and serve:** Remove the fillets from the heat and place them on a warmed serving plate. Lightly cover with aluminum foil and let rest for 5 minutes. The salmon will continue cooking as it rests. Sprinkle with dill and serve with lemon wedges.

*   *Allow one salmon fillet of approximately 6-8 oz (170-225 g) per person.*

** *Montreal Steak Spice is a seasoning blend typically made of salt, black pepper, red pepper, garlic, onion, paprika and sunflower oil. Buy it in supermarkets across Canada and the United States, as well as in a few fine food stores in France and in Belgium, or make your own using one of the many recipes on the Internet.*

GRILLED SWORDFISH
WITH SALSA VERDE

More than 3 hours

serves 4

Summer is when we like to spend time on our terrace and cook on the barbecue. One of our favourite dishes to make is grilled marinated swordfish. There's an interesting flavour conversation happening between the lime-marinated swordfish and the cilantro-packed salsa verde served on the side. We invite some friends over, often Gary and Linda because they love this dish, we have a glass of white wine or a margarita, and life is good.

	MARINADE	
2 tbsp	olive oil	30 mL
2 tbsp	freshly squeezed lime juice	30 mL
2 tsp	lime zest	10 mL
¼ cup	cilantro leaves, chopped	60 mL or 8 g
	SWORDFISH	
4 or 1½-2 lb	swordfish steaks*	4 or 675-900 g
	salt and pepper	
1	lime, in wedges	1

1. **Make the marinade:** In a small bowl, combine the olive oil, lime juice, lime zest and cilantro and mix. Reserve.

2. **Prepare the swordfish:** Put the swordfish steaks in a dish and pat them dry with paper towels. Pour in the marinade and season with salt and pepper. Turn the steaks over so that they are well coated with the marinade. Cover and refrigerate for 2 to 4 hours. Remove from the refrigerator approximately 30 minutes before cooking.

3. **Make the Salsa Verde** while the swordfish marinates. See page 89.

4. **Start up the barbecue**:** Preheat the barbecue to a high temperature (450 ˚F or 232 ˚C), and close the cover.

5. **Cook the swordfish:** When the barbecue is ready, brush and oil the grill. Place the steaks on the grill. Close the cover and grill each side, undisturbed, for 8 to 10 minutes, or until the outside is browned and the inside is cooked (145 ˚F or 63 ˚C). The cooking time will depend on the thickness of the steaks.

6. **Serve:** Remove the steaks from the barbecue and place them on a warmed serving plate. Lightly cover with aluminum foil and let rest for 5 to 8 minutes. Serve with the Salsa Verde.

* *Allow one steak of approximately 6-8 oz (170-225 g) per person.*
** *The swordfish steaks can also be cooked in a grill pan on the stove.*

salsa verde

serves 4 to 6

In 30 minutes

When my sister Élise and my brother-in-law Martin were recipe-hunting on the Internet, they came across a sauce called "Creamy Mexican Chimichurri". I adapted it* to serve with my grilled swordfish steaks. I renamed it Salsa Verde because the cilantro makes it a vivid green. While I love cilantro's fresh bright flavour, others hate it because to them it tastes like soap, apparently something that has to do with their genes. Did I mention it's spicy too? Play it safe and serve your guests the Salsa Verde on the side.

½	medium white onion, coarsely chopped	½
2-3	garlic cloves	2-3
1 cup	cilantro leaves, packed	240 mL or 30 g
2-4 tbsp	freshly squeezed lime juice	30-60 mL
½ cup	extra-virgin olive oil, or avocado oil	120 mL
1 tsp	sea salt	5 mL
3-4 dashes	green Tabasco sauce**	3-4 dashes

1. **Chop the onion and garlic** in a food processor by pulsing a few times.

2. **Make the salsa:** Add the cilantro, lime juice, oil, sea salt and Tabasco, and purée at high speed, until the sauce is smooth. This yields about 1 cup (240 mL) of salsa.

3. **Chill and serve:** Refrigerate the salsa before serving.

4. **Store:** Salsa Verde will keep in the refrigerator for 1 to 2 days.

*　*The original recipe had 5 garlic cloves, and no Tabasco sauce.*
** *For a spicier seasoning, add 1-2 tsp (5-10 mL) of minced jalapeño.*

stews and casseroles
make them ahead of time and you can be part of the party

CHICKEN MARENGO
serves 6 to 8

About 1 to 3 hours

Travel broadens the mind, and the palate too. Surprisingly, it was on my first trip to Italy when I was 18 that I discovered this classic French dish. Marengo is the village in Piedmont where Napoleon defeated the Austrians in 1800, and the story goes that his chef created the dish to celebrate his victory. True or false, what is a fact is that this flavoursome stew made with chicken or veal is always simmered in a sauce with tomatoes, mushrooms, white wine, garlic and olive oil. I turned to Margo Oliver's cookbook Perspectives — Les Menus *for my recipe*. Each time I make this dish, happy memories flood back of my younger days.*

	CHICKEN	
2½–3 lb	chicken breasts, boneless and skinless	1.1–1.4 kg
½ cup	olive oil	120 mL
	VEGETABLES AND SAUCE	
8 oz	white mushrooms, sliced	225 g
12-15	small pearl onions, peeled	12-15
1	green pepper, in strips	1
2 tbsp	unsalted butter	30 mL or 30 g
2 tbsp	all-purpose flour	30 mL or 18 g
1 can of 14 oz	diced tomatoes	1 can of 398 g
2	garlic cloves, minced	2
¼ tsp each	dried oregano and dried basil	1 mL each
¼ cup	chopped fresh parsley, curly or flat	60 mL or 8 g
2 cups	dry white wine	475 mL
	salt and pepper	

1. **Prepare the chicken:** On a cutting board, cut the chicken into 1-inch (2.5 cm) cubes and reserve.

2. **Brown the chicken:** Divide the chicken cubes into 3 or 4 batches. In a Dutch oven, brown each batch in olive oil over medium-high heat. Cook for 2 minutes while stirring, or until the pieces of chicken are lightly browned. With a perforated spoon, transfer the chicken to a bowl. Adjust the heat if needed and repeat with each batch. Reserve.

3. **Cook the mushrooms:** In the same Dutch oven, cook the mushrooms in the chicken cooking juices over low heat for 3 minutes. Remove and reserve.

4. **Cook the vegetables:** Add the onions and the green pepper to the Dutch oven and cook over medium-low heat for 5 minutes, or until the vegetables are lightly browned. Add the butter and let it melt before sprinkling with flour. Stir with a wooden spoon for 2 minutes to cook the flour. Add the tomatoes with their liquid, garlic, oregano, basil and parsley. Season with salt and pepper. Pour in the white wine and deglaze the bottom of the Dutch oven by scraping with the wooden spoon.

5. **Assemble and cook:** Return the chicken to the Dutch oven, cover and cook over medium-low heat for 45 minutes. Uncover and let simmer for 15 to 20 minutes over low heat to reduce the sauce.

6. **Serve:** Add the cooked mushrooms, taste and adjust the seasoning. Chicken Marengo goes well with rice or pasta, and with Spinach Italian-Style (page 63).

7. **Store:** This dish will keep in the refrigerator for 3 to 4 days or in the freezer for 2 to 3 months.

* *Margo Oliver's recipe used 3 medium tomatoes, peeled, seeded and diced, 1 garlic clove and 1½ cups of dry white wine. One cup of rice was added directly into the stew.*

93

Tarragon Chicken
serves 4 to 6

Less than one hour

One spring night, in the charming town of La Jolla in California, Michel and I decided that we would take a cooking class instead of going out to eat. We made our way to Sur la Table, the boutique where chef Gabriel Ferguson was giving his "Date Night: Passport to Paris" class with Tarragon Chicken as the main dish. His version of the well-known classic French dish reintroduced me to tarragon, an aromatic herb that is often forgotten. This is his recipe which I adapted by doubling the sauce . . . because it's all about the sauce!

	CHICKEN	
1½-2 lb	chicken breasts or thighs, boneless, skinless	675 g–900 kg
	sea salt and black pepper	
2 tbsp	olive oil	30 mL
	SAUCE	
2 tbsp	unsalted butter	30 mL or 30 g
2	medium shallots, diced	2
2	garlic cloves, minced	2
½ cup	dry white wine	120 mL
1 cup	chicken broth	240 mL
½ cup	35% cream	120 mL
2 tsp	Dijon mustard	10 mL
¼ cup	chopped fresh tarragon	60 mL or 8 g
2 tsp	freshly squeezed lemon juice	10 mL

1. **Prepare the chicken:** Put the pieces of chicken on a plate and pat them dry with paper towels. Season with salt and pepper.

2. **Brown the chicken:** Divide the chicken pieces into 2 or 3 batches. In a Dutch oven, brown each batch of chicken in olive oil over medium-high heat. Cook for 2 minutes without stirring and continue cooking until the chicken is browned. With a perforated spoon, transfer the chicken to a bowl. Adjust the heat as needed and repeat with each batch. Reserve.

3. **Make the sauce:** In the same Dutch oven, melt the butter over medium-low heat. Add the shallots and garlic and cook for 1 to 2 minutes. Add the white wine and deglaze the bottom by scraping with a wooden spoon. Let simmer for 6 to 8 minutes, or until the wine is almost all reduced. Reducing the wine is important for the sauce to thicken in the next step.

4. Add the chicken broth, cream, mustard and tarragon. Simmer over medium-low heat for 8 to 10 minutes, or until the sauce thickens. Add the lemon juice, taste and adjust the seasoning. If the sauce becomes too thick, add a bit of wine or cream.

5. **Assemble and cook:** Return the chicken to the Dutch oven, let simmer uncovered over low heat for 15 to 20 minutes, or until the chicken is cooked.

6. **Serve:** Transfer the chicken to a warmed serving platter and spoon the sauce over. If desired, serve with rice, carrots or asparagus.

7. **Store:** This dish will keep in the refrigerator for 2 to 3 days.

veal and vegetables
serves 8

About 1 to 3 hours

Because this comforting stew is easy to make and keeps well in the refrigerator or freezer, it's perfect for a family dinner or when entertaining company. In this dish, the veal is browned with pancetta and then simmered with vegetables in a light cream sauce. Served with rice or pasta, garnished with dill and toasted pine nuts, it's pure delight. My mother picked up the recipe at the grocery store several years ago, and since then, my sister-in-law Diane has made it a staple for her family dinners. Try it; it may become a staple in your home, too.

MEAT		
5 oz	pancetta, in ⅜-inch (1 cm) dice	140 g
3 lb	veal, in 1-inch (2.5 cm) cubes	1.4 kg
VEGETABLES AND SAUCE		
4 tbsp	unsalted butter	60 mL or 60 g
2	medium onions, chopped	2
1	leek, white and light green parts, thinly sliced	1
2	garlic cloves, minced	2
3	medium carrots, sliced	3
3 cups or 12 oz	sliced fresh mushrooms	700 mL or 340 g
¼ cup	chopped fresh flat parsley	60 mL or 8 g
1	bouquet garni*	1
	salt and pepper	
2 cups	chicken broth	475 mL
1½ tbsp	unsalted butter, softened	22 mL or 22 g
1½ tbsp	all-purpose flour	22 mL or 12 g
½ cup	35% cream	120 mL
GARNISH		
¼ cup	chopped fresh dill fronds	60 mL or 8 g
	pine nuts, toasted	

1. **Brown the pancetta:** In a Dutch oven, cook the pancetta over medium heat for 5 to 8 minutes, or until it is browned and crisp. With a perforated spoon, transfer the pancetta to a plate lined with paper towels. Reserve.

2. **Brown the veal:** Divide the veal cubes into 3 or 4 batches. In the same Dutch oven, brown each batch of veal in the pancetta-flavoured oil over medium-high heat. Cook for 2 minutes, without stirring, and continue cooking until the cubes are nicely browned. With a perforated spoon, transfer the veal to a bowl. Adjust the heat as needed and repeat with each batch. Reserve.

3. **Brown the vegetables:** In the same Dutch oven, add 4 tbsp (60 mL or 60 g) of the butter and brown the onions, leek, garlic, carrots and mushrooms over medium-high heat for 4 to 5 minutes.

4. **Assemble and cook:** Return the pancetta and the veal to the Dutch oven. Add the parsley, bouquet garni, salt and pepper. Stir. Pour in the chicken broth and bring to a boil. Reduce the heat to low, cover and simmer for 1½ to 2 hours, or until the veal is very tender and pulls apart easily. After this step, the dish will keep in the refrigerator for 3 to 4 days or in the freezer for 2 to 3 months.

5. **Thicken the stew:** In a small bowl, combine the softened butter with the flour and blend into a smooth paste. Add to the stew, stir well and cook for a few minutes, or until the sauce thickens. Warm up the cream without boiling it and add to the sauce. Stir, taste and adjust the seasoning.

6. **Serve** on warmed plates and sprinkle with the dill and toasted pine nuts.

* *Bouquet garni is the name for a bundle of fresh herbs, usually thyme, parsley and bay leaf, tied together in a "bouquet". It is also available dried in a jar or in a sachet at grocery stores.*

Gourmet CHILI
WITH cornbread
serves 8 to 10

About 1 to 3 hours

An image is worth a thousand words: the photo on the cover page of Food & Drink, *the LCBO (Liquor Control Board of Ontario) magazine for winter 2008, was mouth-watering. It featured "Pork 'N' Beans Chili Mole", a hearty dish of pork tenderloin and a side of corn bread. It certainly got my attention. As I gathered the ingredients to make the chili, I decided to replace the dry beans with canned beans, and to double the amount of dark chocolate. My niece Catherine and her partner Félix, confirmed chili-and-corn-bread aficionados, now swear by this recipe.*

	MEAT	
2¼-3 lb	pork tenderloin, in ½-inch (1.25 cm) cubes	1.125-1.4 kg
3 tbsp	coconut oil or olive oil	45 mL
	VEGETABLES AND SAUCE	
2 cups	chopped onions	475 mL or 260 g
2	garlic cloves, minced	2
3 tbsp	chili powder	45 mL
1 tsp	ground cumin	5 mL
½ tsp	salt	2.5 mL
2 cans of 14 oz	diced tomatoes	2 cans of 398 g
1 cup	beef or chicken broth	240 mL
3 cups	ready-made salsa, medium or spicy	700 mL
2 cans of 14 oz	kidney beans, drained and rinsed	2 cans of 398 g
2 oz	unsweetened dark chocolate, in chunks	60 g
3 cups or 12 oz	sliced fresh mushrooms	700 mL or 340 g
½ cup	chopped cilantro leaves	120 mL or 15 g
	GARNISH	
4 cups	shredded Cheddar cheese	950 mL or 480 g
2 cups	sour cream	475 mL
5-6	fresh tomatoes, diced	5-6
4-6	green onions, sliced	4-6
3	limes, in quarters (optional)	3

1. **Brown the meat:** Divide the pork cubes into 3 or 4 batches. In a Dutch oven, brown each batch of pork in the olive oil over medium-high heat. Cook for 2 minutes, without stirring, and continue cooking until the cubes are lightly browned. With a perforated spoon, transfer the pork to a bowl. Adjust the heat as needed and repeat with each batch. Reserve.

2. **Cook the vegetables:** In the same Dutch oven, in the pork cooking juices, cook the onions, garlic and spices for 4 to 5 minutes, or until the onions are softened. Add the diced tomatoes with their juice, the broth and salsa. Stir.

3. **Cook the meat with the vegetables:** Return the pork to the Dutch oven and bring to a boil, stirring frequently. Reduce the heat to low, cover partially and simmer for about 1½ hours, stirring occasionally, or until the pork is well done and pulls apart easily. Add the kidney beans and simmer uncovered for another 30 minutes.

4. **Make the cornbread** while the stew simmers. See page 101.

5. **Assemble and serve:** Add the dark chocolate, mushrooms and cilantro, and stir. Taste and adjust the seasoning as needed. If the chili is too thick, add more broth. Put the chili in warmed bowls topped with shredded cheese. Serve the sour cream, tomatoes, green onions and limes (optional) on the side. Serve with warm corn bread.

6. **Store:** The chili will keep in the refrigerator for 2 to 3 days or in the freezer for 2 to 3 months.

cornbread
makes 16 squares

1½ cups	buttermilk	350 mL
1	large egg, at room temperature	1
¼ cup	granulated sugar	60 mL or 50 g
1 cup	frozen corn kernels	240 mL or 130 g
1 cup	fine cornmeal	240 mL or 135 g
1½ cups	all-purpose flour	350 mL or 180 g
2 tsp	baking powder	10 mL or 10 g
½ tsp	baking soda	2.5 mL or 3 g
¾ tsp	salt	4 mL or 3 g
⅓ cup	unsalted butter, melted	80 mL or 75 g

1. **Prepare the oven and baking pan:** Place the oven rack in the middle position and preheat the oven to 400 °F (200 °C). Butter an 8-inch (20 cm) square baking pan* and line with parchment paper, leaving an overhang on two sides.

2. **Prepare the batter:** In a blender, combine the buttermilk, egg, sugar and frozen corn kernels and blend until the texture is almost smooth.

3. Put the cornmeal in a bowl, add the buttermilk mixture and mix. Let rest for a few minutes, or until the cornmeal is well soaked. Reserve.

4. In a large bowl, sift the flour with the baking powder, baking soda and salt. Make a well in the centre and pour in the buttermilk mixture. Stir lightly with a wooden spoon to wet the flour. Pour in the melted butter and mix until the flour is just incorporated. The batter should be thick and lumpy.

5. **Bake:** Pour the batter in the baking pan and bake for 25 to 30 minutes, or until the cornbread is cooked and lightly browned, and a toothpick inserted in the centre comes out clean.

6. **Cool and serve:** Transfer to a wire rack to cool for 6 to 8 minutes. Turn out the cornbread, remove the parchment paper and let cool on the wire rack completely before cutting into 16 squares. Serve warm or at room temperature.

7. **Store:** Cornbread is best on the day it is made. It will keep in the freezer for 1 to 2 months.

* For a bit of variety, make the cornbread in different baking pans, such as loaf pans or muffin pans.

The Chili as featured on the Winter 2008 issue of the LCBO magazine Food & Drink.

MOUSSAKA

About 1 to 3 hours

serves 4 to 6

Moussaka is a popular dish in Greece, just as shepherd's pie is in Québec. Typically, moussaka is a baked dish made with layers of ground lamb in tomato sauce alternating with layers of eggplant then covered with a white sauce. I discovered eggplant at age 16 when my boyfriend at the time invited me to his home for supper and his mother served moussaka. Since then, I tested and tweaked many moussaka recipes before devising this one, to the great delight of my brother-in-law Jozef.

	EGGPLANT	
1	medium eggplant	1
2 tsp	salt	10 mL
4 tbsp	olive oil	60 mL
	MEAT AND TOMATO SAUCE	
1	medium onion, finely chopped	1
1 lb	ground lamb (or beef)	454 g
6 oz	tomato paste	170 g
	salt and pepper	
pinch of each	ground cinnamon, nutmeg and cloves	pinch of each
⅛ tsp	dried thyme	0.5 mL
1 tsp	dried oregano	5 mL
½ cup	dry red wine	120 mL
2 cups or 8 oz	sliced fresh mushrooms	475 mL or 225 g
	WHITE SAUCE AND TOPPING	
1 cup	5% plain Greek yogourt	240 mL
2	large egg yolks	2
2 tbsp	all-purpose flour	30 mL or 16 g
½ cup	crumbled feta cheese	120 mL or 70 g
2-3 tbsp	breadcrumbs	30-45 mL or 20-30 g

1. **Prepare the eggplant:** Cut the unpeeled eggplant into ⅜-inch (1 cm) thick round slices. Salt both sides of each slice and place in a salad spinner. Let drain for 30 minutes. Spin to remove the accumulated liquid and some of the salt. Put on a plate and pat each slice dry with paper towels.

2. **Cook the eggplant:** In a large frying pan, cook a few eggplant slices in 2-3 tbsp (45 ml) of olive oil over medium heat for 7 to 10 minutes, or until they are browned on both sides. Transfer to a plate lined with paper towels. Repeat with the remaining slices. Reserve.

3. **Prepare the oven:** Place the oven rack in the middle position and preheat the oven to 325 °F (160 °C).

4. **Make the meat and tomato sauce:** In the same frying pan, soften the onion in the remaining olive oil. Add the meat and brown, stirring from time to time. Add the tomato paste and ¾ cup (180 mL) of water. Stir and simmer for 5 minutes. Add the seasoning, wine and mushrooms. Stir and simmer over medium-low heat for 5 to 8 minutes, or until the sauce thickens. Reserve.

5. **Make the white sauce:** In a bowl, beat together with a fork the yogourt, egg yolks and flour until the sauce is smooth.

6. **Assemble:** Cover the bottom of an 8-cup (2 L) baking dish with a layer of the meat and tomato sauce. Top with one layer of eggplant slices. Repeat a second time with the meat and tomato sauce and finish with the eggplant slices. Spread the white sauce evenly over the eggplant. Sprinkle with crumbled feta cheese and breadcrumbs.

7. **Bake** in the oven for about 45 minutes, or until the top is golden brown.

8. **Serve and store:** Let cool for 10 minutes. Serve with a green salad. Moussaka will keep in the refrigerator for 2 to 3 days or in the freezer for 2 to 3 months.

103

Turkey Pot Pie
for a Crowd
serves 12 to 14 *

More than 3 hours

This is my mother's top family-pleasing dish and ranks as my sister-in-law Diane's, my sister Catherine's and my niece Charlotte's all-time favourite. But it comes at a price because it takes a good 5 to 6 hours to make. To make it more manageable, it's best to divide and conquer, and attack the pie in four steps. Start with the broth and the meat, then the vegetables, follow up with the béchamel sauce, finishing off with the pie crust and baking the pie. Did I mention that the sage-flavoured pie crust is exceptional? This recipe comes from Margo Oliver's 1977 book Perspectives — Cuisine de choix, with two changes. There is no dried chervil because it's hard to find, and the cooked ham strips are gone because I don't like mixing the taste of pork with the taste of turkey. Bon appétit!

STEP 1: Broth and Meat

8 lb	whole turkey, cut up**	3.6 kg
2	large carrots, roughly chopped	2
2	celery stalks, with leaves, roughly chopped	2
1	medium onion, peeled, studded with 6 cloves	1
6	large bunches of fresh curly parsley	6
12	black peppercorns	12
1	bay leaf	1
4 tsp	salt	20 mL

1. **Make the broth:** In a large stockpot of 16 cups (4 L), put the cut-up turkey pieces and cover with cold water. Add the carrots, celery, onion studded with cloves, parsley, peppercorns, bay leaf and salt.

2. Cover and cook the turkey and vegetables over high heat and bring to a boil. Reduce the heat to low, cover and simmer for 2 to 3 hours, or until the turkey is just tender. Remove the turkey pieces from the stockpot and let cool. Reserve.

3. Pour the broth through a strainer over a bowl large enough to hold approximately 14 cups (3.5 L) of broth. Let cool and refrigerate. Reserve the broth for Step 2: Vegetables, and Step 3: Béchamel Sauce.

4. **Prepare the meat:** Debone the turkey pieces and cut the meat into bite-sized portions. There should be about 10 cups (2.4 L) of meat. Put in a bowl, wrap in plastic and refrigerate. Reserve for assembling at the end of Step 2: Vegetables.

5. **Store:** The broth and the meat pieces will keep in the refrigerator for 2 to 3 days or in the freezer for 2 to 3 months.

---

* *The whole recipe (the 4 steps) can be cut in half to make 6 to 7 servings.*
** *The recipe is just as good with chicken.*

STEP 2: VEGETABLES

¼ cup	unsalted butter	60 mL or 56 g
16 oz	fresh mushrooms, sliced	454 g
2 cups	turkey broth from Step 1	475 mL
12	medium carrots, thinly sliced	12
1	head of celery, thinly sliced diagonally	1
3 tsp	salt	15 mL
½ tsp	pepper	2.5 mL
2 tsp	dried thyme	10 mL
1 tsp	dried marjoram	5 mL
1 cup	chopped fresh curly parsley	240 mL or 30 g
10 cups	cooked turkey meat from Step 1	2.4 L

1. **Cook the mushrooms:** In a frying pan, brown the mushrooms in the butter over low heat for 5 minutes while stirring. Remove from the heat, put in a bowl and reserve.

2. **Cook the vegetables:** In a large saucepan, bring the turkey broth to a boil over high heat. Add the carrots and celery and bring to a boil. Reduce the heat to medium-low, cover and cook for 10 minutes, or until the vegetables are al dente. Drain in a strainer above a large bowl to reserve the cooking liquid for Step 3: Béchamel Sauce.

3. **Mix the seasoning:** In a small bowl, combine the salt, pepper, thyme, marjoram and fresh parsley.

4. **Assemble:** In two baking dishes of 8-by-12 inches (20 cm by 30 cm), start with a layer of turkey, follow with a layer of mushrooms and a layer of vegetables. Sprinkle with half of the seasoning mix. Repeat one more time.

5. **Store:** If the preparation of the Béchamel Sauce (Step 3) is postponed, wrap the baking dishes in plastic and refrigerate.

STEP 3: BÉCHAMEL SAUCE

1 cup	unsalted butter	240 mL or 225 g
1 cup	chopped onion	240 mL or 130 g
1 cup	all-purpose flour	240 mL or 120 g
6 cups	vegetable cooking liquid and turkey broth	1.4 L
2 tsp	salt	10 mL
¼ tsp	pepper	1 mL
¼ tsp	nutmeg, ground or freshly grated	1 mL
1 tbsp	freshly squeezed lemon juice	15 mL
2 cups	15% cream	475 mL

1. **Cook the onion:** In a large saucepan, cook the onion in butter over low heat and stir for 3 minutes, or until the onion is softened.

2. **Make the sauce:** Sprinkle with flour and cook for 1-2 minutes while stirring with a whisk until it starts to bubble. Remove from the heat, add the reserved vegetable cooking liquid and turkey broth all at once and mix well. Add the salt, pepper and nutmeg. Return to the heat and continue to cook, while stirring, until the sauce starts to bubble and is smooth and thick. While stirring over low heat, add the lemon juice and cream and mix.

3. **Assemble and store:** Pour half of the sauce into each baking dish from Step 2. Let it cool.

4. Wrap the baking dishes in plastic and refrigerate for one day, or proceed to the next step.

1	egg yolk	1
1 tbsp	cold water	15 mL
2 cups	all-purpose flour, sifted	475 mL or 230 g
1 tsp	salt	5 mL
2 tsp	sage	10 mL
¾ cup	chilled shortening, in cubes*	180 mL or 145 g
¼ cup	ice water	60 mL

1. **Prepare the oven:** Place the oven rack in the middle position and preheat the oven to 400 °F (200 °C).

2. **Make the egg wash:** In a small bowl, beat the egg yolk and cold water together with a fork. Reserve.

3. **Make the dough:** In a large bowl, mix the flour with the salt and sage. Cut the shortening cubes into the flour mixture using a pastry cutter, or two knives, until they are the size of small peas. Slowly add the water and gently stir with a fork until the dough starts to come together. The mixture will be a bit dry and crumbly.

4. **Shape and chill the dough:** On a work surface, use your hands to press the dough gently into a ball. Turn and press the ball 3 or 4 times to blend in any dry bits. Flatten into a thick disk and wrap tightly in plastic. Let rest in the refrigerator for at least one hour. If not using right away, refrigerate for up to 3 days, or freeze for up to a month. Thaw in the refrigerator overnight before using.

5. **Roll out the dough:** Remove the dough disk from the refrigerator. Divide it in half. Use your hands to shape each half disk into a full disk.

6. Lightly flour a work surface and a rolling pin. Place one of the dough disks in the centre of the work surface. Roll it outward from its centre in all directions. Gently lift up the dough and rotate about a quarter turn several times. As needed, flour the work surface and the rolling pin to prevent the dough from sticking. Keep rolling out the dough until it is approximately 9-by-13 inches (23 cm by 33 cm), or large enough to cover the top of the baking dish, with an overhang of about ½ inch (1.25 cm) all around. Repeat with the second dough disk.

7. **Cover the pies:** Cover each baking dish from Step 3 with the rolled-out dough and trim the edges with a knife, as needed. Tuck the overhanging dough underneath itself, and then lightly press the dough rim on the lip of the baking dish. With a knife, cut a few openings into the dough to let the steam escape during cooking. With a pastry brush, baste the dough with the egg wash, without touching the edges.

8. **Bake the pies and serve:** Bake in the oven for 1 hour, or until the sauce bubbles and the tops are nicely browned. Serve hot, with a green salad as a side dish.

9. **Store:** When cooked, the turkey pot pie will keep in the freezer for 2 to 3 months.

* Use Crisco shortening or replace it with ⅔ cup (170 mL) of cooking lard.

cookies and squares
STICKY FINGERS Guaranteed

OLD-FASHIONED OaTMEAL COOKIES

MAKES 48 COOKIES

Less than one hour

Some cookies are timeless, and some cookies are family favourites. These cookies are both and they happen to be my mother's favourite. My sisters, my brothers and I loved eating them as we grew up, and even now, we continue our childhood habit of eating them straight out of the cookie box when we visit our mother. Enjoy these old-fashioned soft cookies with fresh fruit or homemade apple sauce.

1 cup or ½ lb	unsalted butter, softened*	240 mL or 225 g
1½ cups	brown sugar	350 mL or 300 g
2	large eggs, at room temperature	2
½ cup	buttermilk**	120 mL
1¾ cups	all-purpose flour	420 mL or 210 g
1 tsp	baking soda	5 mL or 6 g
1 tsp	baking powder	5 mL or 5 g
1 tsp	salt	5 mL or 5 g
1 tsp	ground cinnamon	5 mL
1 tsp	nutmeg, ground or freshly grated	5 mL
3 cups	old-fashioned rolled oats	700 mL or 270 g
1 cup	raisins	240 mL or 140 g
½ cup	chopped walnuts	120 mL or 75 g

1. **Prepare the oven and cookie sheets:** Place the oven rack in the top third position and preheat the oven to 400 °F (200 °C). Line two large cookie sheets with parchment paper.

2. **Make the dough:** In a large bowl, cream together the butter, brown sugar and eggs with a wooden spoon, or an electric mixer at medium speed, until the mixture is smooth. Add the buttermilk and mix.

3. In a small bowl, sift together the flour, baking soda, baking powder, salt, cinnamon and nutmeg. Combine with the butter mixture and incorporate with a wooden spoon, or an electric mixer at low speed, until the ingredients are just combined. Add the rolled oats, raisins and walnuts, and mix with the wooden spoon. If not baking right away, keep the cookie dough in the refrigerator for 2 to 3 days or in the freezer for 2 to 3 months.

4. **Shape the cookies:** With a medium ice cream or cookie scoop (1½ tbsp or 22.5 mL), scoop out 48 cookies and place them about 2 inches (5 cm) apart on the cookie sheets. The cookies will keep their shape while cooking.

5. **Bake** in the oven for 8 to 10 minutes, or until the cookies are just turning golden brown. The cookies will continue to cook a little after they come out of the oven. If your oven can't hold two cookie sheets at a time, repeat with the second cookie sheet.

6. **Cool and store:** Transfer each cookie sheet to a wire rack and let the cookies cool completely. Store the cookies in an airtight container at room temperature for 5 to 7 days or in the freezer for 5 to 6 months.

* *Old-fashioned cookie recipes often use shortening instead of butter.*
** *The buttermilk can be replaced by ½ cup (120 mL) of whole milk + ¼ tsp (1 mL) of baking soda + 2 tsp (10 mL or 10 g) of baking powder.*

Mariette's
Chocolate Chip Cookies
Makes 48 Cookies

Less than one hour

This recipe was given to me by Mariette Rousseau-Vermette, an internationally known Québec tapestry artist. When I worked as an architect at Arthur Erickson's firm for the construction of Roy Thomson Hall in the early 1980s, she had been commissioned to design the concert hall ceiling. I had become friends with her son Marc and was invited several times to her home in Ste-Adèle. During my visits, she would offer me her chocolate chip cookies with a cup of tea. Treasured moments.

1 cup or ½ lb	unsalted butter, softened	240 mL or 225 g
1½ cups	brown sugar	350 mL or 300 g
2	large eggs, at room temperature	2
2 cups	whole wheat flour	475 mL or 250 g
1 tsp	baking soda	5 mL or 6 g
½ tsp	salt	2.5 mL or 2.5 g
1 tsp	vanilla	2.5 mL
½ cup	unsweetened shredded coconut	120 mL or 45 g
1 cup or more	semi-sweet chocolate chips	240 mL or 180 g, or more
¼ cup	unsalted sunflower seeds, or chopped pecans	60 mL or 35 g

1. **Prepare the oven and cookie sheets:** Place the oven rack in the top third position and preheat the oven to 325 °F (160 °C). Line two large cookie sheets with parchment paper.

2. **Make the dough:** In a large bowl, cream together the butter, brown sugar and eggs with a wooden spoon, or an electric mixer at medium speed, until the mixture is smooth.

3. In a small bowl, sift together the flour, baking soda and salt. Combine with the butter mixture and incorporate with a wooden spoon, or an electric mixer at low speed, until the ingredients are just combined. Add the vanilla, shredded coconut, chocolate chips, and sunflower seeds or chopped pecans. Mix with the wooden spoon. If not baking right away, keep the cookie dough in the refrigerator for 2 to 3 days or in the freezer for 2 to 3 months.

4. **Shape the cookies:** With a medium ice cream or cookie scoop (1½ tbsp or 22.5 mL), scoop out 48 cookies and place them about 2 inches (5 cm) apart on the cookie sheets. The cookies will spread a bit while cooking.

5. **Bake** in the oven for 8 to 10 minutes, or until the cookies are just turning golden brown. The cookies will continue to cook a little after they come out of the oven. If your oven can't hold two cookie sheets at a time, repeat with the second cookie sheet.

6. **Cool and store:** Transfer each cookie sheet to a wire rack and let the cookies cool completely. Store the cookies in an airtight container at room temperature for 5 to 7 days or in the freezer for 5 to 6 months.

Walnut Brownies
makes 16 squares or 24 mini-brownies

Are you a chocoholic? If yes, these brownies will satisfy your addiction. The recipe was given to my mother by Ida, her dear friend Thérèse's devoted cook in the early 1950s. My mother made these brownies almost every week for 20 years, until I started making them late at night for my brother Pierre and his college friends. Morning, noon or night, these walnut brownies tend to disappear like hot cakes.

2-4 oz	baking chocolate, unsweetened (100% cacao)	60-115 g
½ cup	unsalted butter	120 mL or 115 g
2	large eggs, at room temperature	2
1 cup	granulated sugar	240 mL or 200 g
1 tsp	pure vanilla extract	5 mL
½ cup	all-purpose flour	120 mL or 60 g
½ tsp	baking powder	2.5 mL or 3 g
¼ tsp	salt	1 mL or 1g
½ cup	chopped walnuts	120 mL or 75 g

1. **Prepare the oven and pan:** Place the oven rack in the middle position and preheat the oven to 350 ˚F (180 ˚C). Lightly butter an 8-inch (20 cm) square pan and line with parchment paper, leaving an overhang on two sides.

2. **Melt the chocolate:** In the top part of a double boiler, melt the butter and chocolate over simmering water. Stir the butter and chocolate gently until they have melted. Make sure no water splashes into the chocolate as it will make it seize up and turn grainy. Remove from the heat and cool.

3. **Make the batter:** In a bowl, beat the eggs and the sugar with an electric mixer at medium speed until they are foamy. Add the cooled chocolate and the vanilla. Mix.

4. In another bowl, sift the flour, baking powder and salt together. Combine with the chocolate mixture and incorporate with a wooden spoon until the ingredients are just blended in. Add the walnuts and mix. Pour the batter into the pan.

5. **Bake** in the oven for 20 to 25 minutes, or until the brownies are cooked around the edges but still moist in the centre. The brownies will continue to cook a little after they come out of the oven.

6. **Cool and store:** Transfer to a wire rack to cool for 6 to 8 minutes. Turn out the brownies, remove the parchment paper and let cool on the wire rack completely before cutting into 16 squares. Store the brownies in an airtight container at room temperature for 1 to 2 days or in the freezer for 2 to 3 months.

Variations
• *For less fudgy brownies, use ¾ cup (180 mL or 90 g) of flour.*
• *To deepen the chocolate flavour, add 1 tsp (5 mL) of instant coffee granules to the melted chocolate in step 2.*
• *If baking the brownies in mini-muffin pans, reduce the baking time to about 15 minutes.*

favourite Date squares
makes 16 Large squares

Date desserts never go out of date and, in our family, aunt Élise is the recognized expert on date squares. When she was a newlywed in 1956, she tested many recipes before declaring this one as THE best. Was it because the American recipe was called matrimonial bars? Just so you know, here in Canada we call it matrimonial cake. What I like about this recipe is that the date filling is just that . . . dates.

	FILLING	
8-12 oz	pitted dates, chopped	225–340 g
1-1½ cups	boiling water	240-350 mL
	OAT CRISP	
1¼ cups	all-purpose flour	300 mL or 150 g
¼ tsp	baking soda	1 mL or 1 g
½ tsp	salt	2.5 mL or 2.5 g
1¼ cups	old-fashioned rolled oats*	300 mL or 115 g
1 cup	brown sugar	240 mL or 200 g
¾ cup	unsalted butter, softened	180 mL or 170 g

1. **Prepare the oven and pan:** Place the oven rack in the middle position and preheat the oven to 375 ˚F (190 ˚C). Lighlty butter an 8-inch (20 cm) square pan and line with parchment paper leaving an overhang on two sides.

2. **Make the filling:** In a saucepan, combine the dates and water and bring to a boil. Reduce the heat, simmer for about 10 minutes while pressing lightly on the dates with a wooden spoon until the dates are softened and the mixture is like a purée. Remove from the heat and cool.

3. **Make the oat crisp:** In a large bowl, sift the flour, baking soda, and salt. Add the rolled oats and brown sugar. Mix. Add the butter and incorporate into the dry ingredients with a pastry cutter or a wooden spoon. The mixture will be a bit dry and crumbly.

4. **Assemble:** Spread a bit more than half of the oat mixture on the bottom of the pan and press down evenly with the back of a spoon or with your hands. Spread the date filling to cover. Crumble the rest of the oat mixture over the date filling and press lightly with your hands.

5. **Bake** in the oven for about 30 minutes, or until the topping is golden brown.

6. **Cool and store:** Transfer to a wire rack to cool for 6 to 8 minutes. Turn out the date dessert, remove the parchment paper, and let cool on the wire rack completely before cutting into 16 squares. Store the date squares in an airtight container at room temperature for 5 to 7 days or in the freezer for 2 to 3 months.

* Do not use quick-cooking oats because they have a bland flavour.

pecan squares
makes 16 Large squares

Some say puh-KAHN; others say PEE-can. Apparently, the word pecan came into the English language from the French, who got it from an Algonquin language. The recipe for these scrumptious pecan squares comes from my grandmother Thérèse, who would serve them cut into dainty squares with coffee in the afternoon. Carrying on her sweet tradition, I've been making them for 40 years and I don't wait for an afternoon coffee break to have them.

	BASE	
½ cup	unsalted butter, softened	120 mL or 115 g
½ cup	brown sugar	120 mL or 100 g
1 cup	all-purpose flour	240 mL or 120 g
	TOPPING	
½ cup	unsweetened shredded cococut	120 mL or 45 g
2 tbsp	all-purpose flour	30 mL or 17 g
2	large eggs, at room temperature	2
1 cup	brown sugar	240 mL or 200 g
1 cup	chopped pecans	240 mL or 120 g
1 tsp	pure vanilla extract	5 mL
pinch	salt	pinch
1 tbsp	icing sugar	15 mL or 7 g

1. **Prepare the oven and pan:** Place the oven rack in the middle position and preheat the oven to 350 °F (180 °C). Lightly butter an 8-inch (20 cm) square pan and line it with parchment paper leaving an overhang on two sides.

2. **Make the base:** In a bowl, cream the butter and brown sugar. Working with a wooden spoon, or an electric mixer at low speed, incorporate the flour until the dough is smooth. Transfer the dough to the pan and cover the bottom by pressing down evenly with your hands.

3. **Bake** in the oven for 10 to 15 minutes, or until the cookie base is golden brown. Transfer to a wire rack to cool. Reserve.

4. **Make the topping:** In the meantime, in a small bowl, mix the coconut with the flour. Reserve.

5. In another bowl, beat the eggs with an electric mixer, increasing from low to high speed, until the eggs are foamy. Gradually add the brown sugar and mix with a wooden spoon until the mixture is smooth. Add the pecans, coconut with flour, vanilla, and salt. Mix and pour on top of the cooled cookie base.

6. **Bake** in the oven for about 15 minutes, or until the topping is golden brown, the edges are cooked but the centre is still a bit runny. It will continue to cook a little after coming out of the oven.

7. **Cool and store:** Transfer to a wire rack to cool for 6 to 8 minutes. Turn out the pecan dessert, remove the parchment paper, and let cool completely on the wire rack. Sprinkle lightly with icing sugar and cut into 16 large squares. Store the pecan squares in an airtight container at room temperature for 5 to 7 days or in the freezer for 2 to 3 months.

one mousse and two creams

CHILLED SWEET CONCOCTIONS

Parisian Chocolate Mousse
serves 6

This chocolate mousse has been a classic Vézina family dessert for over 50 years. First as my father's favourite dessert, prepared lovingly by my mother for many years, this lusciously rich chocolate mousse has become the dessert of choice for family gatherings. Interpreted by Jehane Benoît, the doyenne of Québec cuisine, her recipe is typical of French cuisine. My mother has since passed it down to my niece Lara who makes it to perfection, to the delight of her cousins, especially William, Charles and Chloé.

8 oz	baking chocolate, semi-sweet (56% cocoa)*	225 g
½ cup	granulated sugar	120 mL or 100 g
¼ cup	water	60 mL
5	large eggs, at room temperature	5
1 tsp	pure vanilla extract	5 mL

1. Melt the chocolate: In the top part of a double boiler, melt the chocolate with the granulated sugar and water over simmering water. Stir until the mixture is smooth. Remove from the heat and cool.

2. Separate the eggs by putting the egg yolks in one large bowl and the egg whites in another.

3. Beat the egg yolks with an electric mixer, increasing from low to high speed, until they are foamy. Slowly add about ¼ cup (60 mL) of the chocolate mixture to the egg yolks; this tempers the yolks and prevents them from curdling. Mix with a wooden spoon. Transfer the tempered egg yolks to the chocolate mixture in the double boiler. Stir over low heat for 3 to 4 minutes. Add the vanilla, stir, then remove from the heat and cool. Reserve.

4. Beat the egg whites with an electric mixer, increasing from low to high speed, until they form firm peaks. With a spatula, fold the egg whites into the cooled chocolate mixture until they are just mixed in.

5. Chill and serve: Pour the chocolate mixture into six small 1-cup (240 mL) ramequins or in a 6-cup (1.4 L) serving dish. Refrigerate for 6 to 8 hours before serving. The chocolate mousse is delicious with fresh strawberries or raspberries.

6. Store: The chocolate mousse will keep in the refrigerator for 1 to 2 days.

Variation
- *To cut back on sugar and enhance the chocolate flavour, replace 1-2 oz (29-60 g) of the semi-sweet chocolate (56% cocoa) by unsweetened chocolate (100% cocoa).*

123

maple ice cream
serves 6

More than 3 hours

Finally, an ice cream you can make without an ice cream machine! My grandmother Thérèse gave me this recipe, originally called "Biscuits Tortoni". I could never figure out how maple syrup, so very Québec, found its way to a dessert with an Italian name. Apparently, this divine ice cream was invented in the late 1800s. No one knows the real origin of the name, but we do know it was made with a hot sugar syrup and Italian cookies. In our family, we still call it Biscuits Tortoni, and outside the family we call it maple ice cream, so we don't have to explain. Sweet treats made with Québec maple syrup have no borders — this ice cream won over Michel's daughter Axelle, and my good friend Hélène, both living in Brussels.

3	large eggs, at room temperature	3
1 cup	35% cream	240 mL
¾ cup	maple syrup, dark if available	180 mL
pinch	salt	pinch
½ cup	finely crumbled honey graham crackers*	120 mL or 45 g

1. **Separate the eggs** in 3 bowls: one bowl for the 3 egg yolks, one bowl for 1 egg white, and one bowl for 2 egg whites. Set aside the first two bowls and save the 2 egg whites for another recipe.

2. **Make the maple mixture:** Lightly beat the 3 egg yolks with a whisk. Add ¼ cup (60 mL) of the cream and the maple syrup. Mix until the mixture is blended.

3. Pour the maple syrup mixture into the top part of a double boiler. Cook over simmering water while stirring with a wooden spoon for 15 to 20 minutes, or until the mixture thickens and coats the spoon. This step might seem long, but it's important to make sure that the egg yolks don't scramble. Remove from the heat and cool.

4. **Beat the egg white** with a whisk or an electric mixer, increasing from low to high speed, until it forms firm peaks. Reserve.

5. **Whip the cream:** In another bowl, whip the rest of the cream with an electric mixer, increasing from low to high speed. Fold the egg white into the whipped cream with a spatula. Mix in a pinch of salt and half of the graham crackers. Fold the whipped cream into the maple mixture until just combined.

6. **Freeze:** Pour the maple cream into a stainless-steel bowl, wrap in plastic and put in the freezer for 4 to 6 hours, or until the cream is firm. Remove from the freezer, let rest for about 20 minutes and stir with a wooden spoon to soften the cream. Pour the softened cream into individual ramequins. Freeze for 6 to 8 hours, or overnight until the cream is frozen again.

7. **Serve:** Remove from the freezer and sprinkle with the rest of the graham crackers to serve.

8. **Store:** The maple ice cream will keep in the freezer for 1 to 2 months.

* The honey graham crackers can be replaced by ground almonds, or Spéculoos cookies, well-known Belgian cookies.

125

crème brûlée
WITH WHITE CHOCOLATE AND PISTACHIOS
serves 6

More than 3 hours

L'Express, a very French bistro in Montréal, reimagined crème brûlée with white chocolate and pistachios. My friend Catherine, who was visiting from Toronto, and I were playing tourist in the Plateau Mont-Royal neighbourhood when we decided to stop by and try this intriguing burnt cream. As soon as I closed my eyes to get the full experience of this rich silky custard with a crackly caramelized sugar crust, there was no going back — I had to get the recipe. In the end, I created my own and recently perfected it with my cousin Louise and her daughter Laurence.

3 cups	35% cream	700 mL
6 oz	white chocolate, chips or squares	170 g
2 tbsp	pistachio paste*	30 mL
5	large eggs, at room temperature	5
2 tbsp	granulated sugar	30 mL or 25 g
pinch	salt	pinch
6 tbsp	granulated sugar for the topping	90 mL or 80 g

1. **Prepare the oven and the pan:** Place the oven rack in the middle position and preheat the oven to 300 °F (150 °C). Place six shallow 1-cup (120 mL) ramequins in a large baking pan.

2. **Heat the cream** in a saucepan over medium-low heat until it simmers, just before it gets to boiling. Remove from the heat and add the white chocolate. Gently stir to melt. Add the pistachio cream and mix. Reserve.

3. **Prepare the egg yolks:** Separate 4 of the eggs and put the egg yolks in a mixing bowl. Save the 4 egg whites for another recipe. Add the 5th egg to the egg yolks and whisk. Mix in the sugar and the salt.

4. **Prepare the burnt cream mixture:** Gradually pour the lukewarm cream-chocolate mixture into the eggs while stirring with the whisk until the mixture is smooth. Pour the burnt cream mixture through a strainer placed over a 6-cup (1.4 L) measuring cup. Using the measuring cup, pour the mixture into the ramequins until they are three-quarters full.

5. **Bake in a water bath:** Put the baking pan with the ramequins in the oven. Before closing the oven door, add very hot water to the pan halfway up around the side of the ramequins. Bake for about 30 minutes, or until the cream is set around the edges but is still jiggly in the centre. Do not overcook!

6. **Cool and refrigerate:** Remove the baking pan from the oven and immediately transfer each ramequin to a wire rack so that the cream does not continue to cook in the hot water. Cool for 60 minutes. Wrap each ramequin in plastic and refrigerate for 4 hours, or overnight.

7. **Caramelize and serve:** Before serving, sprinkle white sugar evenly over the surface of each ramequin. Burn the sugar with a kitchen blowtorch by moving the flame continuously about 1 inch (2.5 cm) above the surface until the sugar melts and caramelizes. Do not put the ramequins under the broiler to caramelize the sugar as the heat will overcook the crème brûlée and make it grainy. Serve immediately or within two hours.

8. **Store:** The crème brûlée will keep in the refrigerator for 2 to 3 days or in the freezer for 2 to 3 months.

* Pistachio paste, a sweetened preparation, is sold in fine food stores.

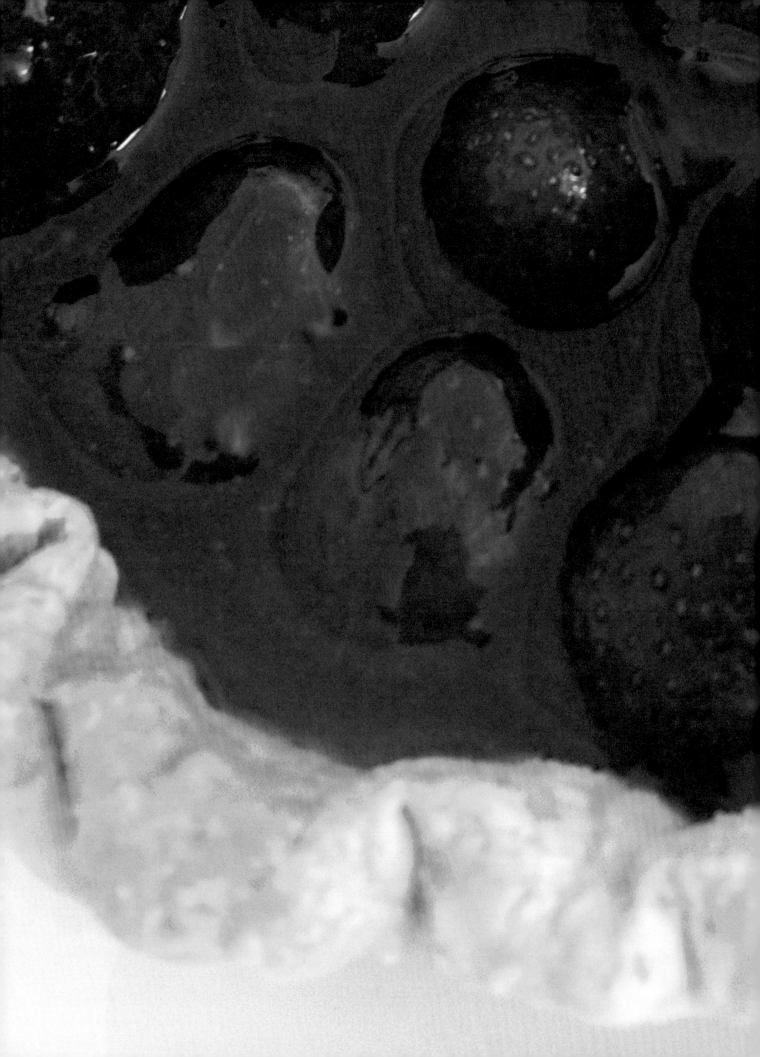

PIES
OLD-FASHIONED AND STILL IN STYLE

CLASSIC PIE DOUGH, or Pâte Brisée

MAKES TWO 9-INCH (23 CM) CRUSTS

Less than one hour

Sitting at the kitchen counter after school, I spent countless hours watching my mother make pies. When she felt I was ready, she let me roll the pastry dough under her supervision, then she watched me make a pie from beginning to end, and finally she let me fly solo. With pie-making from scratch becoming a lost art, it's important to nurture and pass on this culinary tradition. I am delighted to share my family's recipe with you.

1½ cups	all-purpose flour	350 mL or 180 g
⅛ tsp	salt	0.5 mL or 0.6 g
½ cup	vegetable shortening, cold, in 1-inch (2.5 cm) cubes*	120 mL or 95 g
¼ cup	ice water	60 mL

1. **Make the dough:** In a large bowl, sift the flour and mix with the salt. Using a pastry cutter, or two knives, cut the shortening cubes into the flour until they are the size of small peas. Slowly add the water and stir lightly with a fork until the dough just comes together. The mixture will be a little dry and crumbly.

2. On a work surface, use your hands to press the dough gently into a ball. Turn and press the ball 3 or 4 times to blend in any dry bits. Flatten the ball into a thick disk and wrap tightly in plastic. Let rest in the refrigerator for 30 minutes.

3. **Shape the dough:** Divide the chilled dough disk in half. Use your hands to shape each half into a disk. Wrap one of the two disks in plastic and reserve for future use to make a second single-crust pie, a lattice top for a pie, or the top crust for a double-crust pie. If not using right away, refrigerate for 1 week or freeze for 1 to 2 months.

4. **Roll out the dough:** Lightly flour a work surface and a rolling pin. Place the dough disk in the centre of the work surface. Make the disk into a thin circle about 11 to 12 inches (28 to 30 cm) in diameter by rolling outward from its centre in all directions. Gently lift up and rotate the dough about a quarter turn several times. As needed, flour the work surface and the rolling pin to prevent the dough from sticking. Keep rolling until the circle is the right diameter.

5. **Line the pie plate:** Roll the dough loosely over the pin, centre the pin over a 9-inch (23 cm) pie plate and unroll the dough. Loosely ease the dough into the plate, and then press gently on the bottom and sides to fit it into the plate. Allow the excess dough to hang over the edges by about ¾ inch (2 cm). Use a knife to trim the edges. Keep the trimmings to make Brown Sugar Palmier Rolls (page 141).

6. **Make and flute the dough rim for a single-crust pie:** Tuck the overhanging dough underneath itself and rest the rim on the lip of the pie plate. To flute the rim, use the index finger of one hand and the thumb and index finger of the other hand to make ridges perpendicular to the pie plate.

7. **Wrap and store:** Loosely wrap the dough-lined pie plate in plastic. Use right away, refrigerate for 1 week or freeze for 1 to 2 months.

* Use Crisco vegetable shortening, easily available in grocery stores.

Andrée's Lattice-Top Apple Pie

Makes One Double-Crust 9-Inch (23 cm) Pie

About 1 to 3 hours

My mother is Andrée and this is the pie that made her reputation as a star pastry cook among her friends. For Jane Austen, "Good apple pies are a considerable part of our domestic happiness"; for my father, "Apple pie is the queen of pies and the hallmark of an excellent cook." I'm quite sure he was thinking of the talented cook in his life when he made that statement. My brother Louis and my nephew Benjamin are categorical: it's this pie and no other.

	APPLE FILLING	
¾ cup	granulated sugar	180 mL or 150 g
3 tbsp	all-purpose flour	45 mL or 25 g
6-8	Cortland, Granny Smith or McIntosh apples, peeled, cored, thinly sliced	6-8
pinch of each	ground cinnamon and ground nutmeg	pinch of each
	PASTRY*	
1	unbaked 9-inch (23 cm) pie shell in a pie plate	1
1	single-crust pie dough disk	1
1 tbsp	15% or 35% cream	15 mL
pinch	granulated sugar	pinch
1 tbsp	unsalted butter, cold	15 mL or 15 g

1. **Prepare the oven:** Place the oven rack in the bottom position and preheat the oven to 400 °F (200 °C).

2. **Make the apple filling:** In a large bowl, mix the sugar with the flour. Add the apple slices and mix gently to coat. Arrange the apples on the unbaked pie shell so that they fill the shell. The apples will decrease in volume as the pie bakes. Reserve.

3. **Roll out the pastry dough:** Lightly flour a work surface and a rolling pin. Place the dough disk in the centre of the work surface. Make the disk into a thin circle about 11 inches (28 cm) in diameter by rolling outward from its centre in all directions. Gently lift up and rotate the dough about a quarter turn several times. As needed, flour the work surface and the rolling pin to prevent the dough from sticking. Keep rolling until the circle is the right diameter.

4. **Weave the lattice top:** With a knife, cut the circle into 16 strips about ½-inch (1.25 cm) wide. Starting with the longest strips and working from the middle outwards, place one strip down the middle of the filled pie shell. Take another strip and place it perpendicular to the first strip, also down the middle. Continue working this way, away from the middle in opposite directions, by spacing them about ½-inch (1.25 cm) apart. Weave each strip under and over the strips that it crosses. When the lattice is finished, trim off any overhanging dough with a knife, then press the strip ends down gently into the rim of the pie shell.

5. **Brush** the lattice strips with cream using a pastry brush, and sprinkle with sugar. Scatter a few small knobs of butter in the lattice openings.

6. **Bake** in the oven for about 30 minutes at 400 °F (200 °C). Lower the temperature to 350 °F (190 °C) and continue baking for 20 to 25 minutes, or until the apples are softened, the filling is bubbling, and the lattice top is golden brown.

7. **Cool, serve and store:** Transfer to a wire rack to cool. Serve at room temperature. This apple pie is delicious served with vanilla ice cream or whipped cream. It will keep in the refrigerator for 2 to 3 days or in the freezer for 2 to 3 months.

* Use the recipe on page 131 or buy a ready-made unbaked pie shell and dough at the grocery store.

Lattice-Top Raspberry Pie

Makes one Double-Crust 9-inch (23 cm) Pie

About 1 to 3 hours

It's as easy as apple pie, in fact, easier because there is no fruit to peel, core, dice or slice. Honestly, turning out homemade pastry and a lattice top isn't rocket science. You'll love every bite of this pie bursting with the sweet-tart taste of jammy raspberries and lovely flaky pie crust. I could eat it every day, and it really should be called "Anne's Pie."

	RASPBERRY FILLING	
¾ cup	granulated sugar	180 mL or 150 g
3 tbsp	all-purpose flour	45 mL or 25 g
6 cups or 30 oz	raspberries, fresh or frozen, unsweetened	1.4 L or 855 g
	PASTRY*	
1	unbaked 9-inch (23 cm) pie shell in a pie plate	1
1	single-crust pie dough disk	1
1 tbsp	15% or 35% cream	15 mL
pinch	granulated sugar	pinch
1 tbsp	unsalted butter, cold	15 mL or 15 g

1. **Prepare the oven:** Place the oven rack in the bottom position and preheat the oven to 400 °F (200 °C).

2. **Make the raspberry filling:** In a large bowl, mix the sugar with the flour. Add the raspberries and mix gently to coat. Arrange the raspberries on the unbaked pie shell so that they fill the shell. The raspberries will decrease in volume as the pie bakes. Reserve.

3. **Roll out the pastry dough:** Lightly flour a work surface and a rolling pin. Place the dough disk in the centre of the work surface. Make the disk into a thin circle about 11 inches (28 cm) in diameter by rolling it outward from its centre in all directions. Gently lift up and rotate the dough about a quarter turn several times. As needed, flour the work surface and the rolling pin to prevent the dough from sticking. Keep rolling until the circle is the right diameter.

4. **Weave the lattice top:** With a knife, cut the circle into 16 strips of about ½-inch (1.25 cm) wide. Starting with the longest strips and working from the middle outwards, place one strip down the middle of the filled pie shell. Take another strip and place it perpendicular to the first strip, also down the middle. Continue working this way, away from the middle in opposite directions, by spacing them about ½-inch (1.25 cm) apart. Weave each strip under and over the strips that it crosses. When the lattice is finished, trim off any overhanging dough with a knife, then press the strip ends down gently into the rim of the pie shell.

5. **Brush** the lattice strips with cream using a pastry brush, and sprinkle with sugar. Scatter a few small knobs of butter in the lattice open spaces.

6. **Bake** in the oven for about 30 minutes at 400 °F (200 °C). Lower the temperature to 350 °F (190 °C) and continue baking for 20 to 25 minutes, or until the filling is bubbling and the lattice top is golden brown.

7. **Cool, serve and store:** Transfer to a wire rack to cool. Serve at room temperature. This raspberry pie is delicious served with vanilla ice cream or whipped cream. It will keep in the refrigerator for 2 to 3 days or in the freezer for 2 to 3 months.

* Use the recipe on page 131 or buy a ready-made unbaked pie shell and dough at the grocery store.

Variation
• *Use blueberries instead of raspberries.*

GLaZeD STRaWBeRRY TaRT
MaKeS One SINGLe-CRUST 9-INCH (23 CM) PIe

About 1 to 3 hours

Can you imagine a summer without strawberry pies? These days, thanks to late-variety strawberries, you can find local strawberries at farmer's markets and grocery stores from early June to mid-October. My aunt Élise always made her strawberry tarts with a zero-waste mindset. Her recipe transforms ugly strawberries into a syrup that glazes the tart and makes it shine. For my nephew Vincent-Pierre and his sister Charlotte, summer would not be the same without aunt Élise's scrumptious strawberry tart.

1	unbaked 9-inch (23 cm) pie shell in a pie plate*	1
¾ cup	granulated sugar	180 mL or 150 g
3 tbsp	cornstarch	45 mL or 25 g
5-6 dozen	fresh strawberries, hulled	5-6 dozen
¾ cup	water	180 mL
1 tsp	freshly squeezed lemon juice	5 mL

1. **Prepare the oven:** Place the oven rack in the middle position and preheat the oven to 400 °F (200 °C).

2. **Blind bake:** With a fork, poke holes on the surface and sides of the pie shell so the dough won't puff up as it bakes. Bake in the oven for 15 to 20 minutes, or until the crust is golden brown. Transfer to a wire rack to cool.

3. **Assemble:** When the pie shell has cooled, fill it with the nicest strawberries placed side by side with the tips pointing up. Reserve.

4. **Make the strawberry glaze:** Cut up the blemished strawberries. In a saucepan, put 1 cup (240 mL or 165 g) of the cut-up strawberries in the water. Boil over high heat for 3 minutes. Remove from the heat and strain the strawberries over a bowl to collect the cooking liquid.

5. Put the cooking liquid back in the saucepan and add the sugar mixed in with the cornstarch. While stirring constantly with a wooden spoon or a whisk, bring to a boil and cook over medium-low heat for 5 to 8 minutes, or until the liquid is clear and thick. Do not let the bottom burn. Add the lemon juice and mix.

6. **Glaze the pie:** Pour the warm syrup immediately over the strawberry pie, carefully coating each strawberry.

7. **Cool and serve:** Refrigerate for at least one hour before serving. The tart should be eaten the day it's made and it's best eaten on its own!

* Use the recipe on page 131 or buy a ready-made unbaked pie shell at the grocery store.

pecan pie

MAKES ONE SINGLE-CRUST 9-INCH (23 CM) PIE

If eating dessert is sinful, my brother-in-law Martin would tell you that eating pecan pie is worth the penance. The pecan filling is made in the traditional way with corn syrup, brown sugar, butter, a hint of vanilla, and lots of pecans. As the filling recipe is by Jehane Benoît, culinary grande dame in Québec, and the pie dough by my mother, a culinary grande dame at home, you could call this a joint venture by two special women.

½ cup	unsalted butter, softened	120 mL or 115 g
1 cup	brown sugar	240 mL or 200 g
3	large eggs, beaten	3
1 cup	corn syrup	240 mL
1 tsp	vanilla	5 mL
1 cup	whole pecans	240 mL or 120 g
1	unbaked 9-inch (23 cm) pie shell in a pie plate*	1

1. **Prepare the oven:** Place the oven rack in the bottom position and preheat the oven to 375 °F (190 °C).

2. **Make the filling:** In a bowl, cream the butter and brown sugar with a wooden spoon, or an electric mixer at medium speed. Add the eggs, the corn syrup and the vanilla. Mix. Add the pecans and mix in with a wooden spoon, taking care to keep them whole. Pour the mixture into the unbaked pastry shell in a pie plate.

3. **Bake** in the oven for about 40 minutes, or until the top of the pie is golden.

4. **Cool, serve and store:** Transfer to a wire rack to cool. Serve at room temperature, with vanilla ice cream if desired. The pie will keep at room temperature for 2 to 3 days or in the freezer for 2 to 3 months.

* Use the recipe on page 131 or buy a ready-made unbaked pie shell at the grocery store.

Note: *The pie in the picture on the opposite page was made in an 8-by-11-inch (20 cm by 28 cm) rectangular tart pan.*

Brown Sugar Palmier Rolls

Makes 8 to 10 rolls

In 30 minutes

I don't understand why Quebeckers call these sweet buns "pets-de-soeur," literally nuns' farts. Culinary historians have their theories about this. These sweet little bites are just bits of leftover dough rolled up with butter and brown sugar into a spiral, then sliced and baked. While they're not sophisticated, I like to shape them into palmiers, or elephant ears, to make them look like French petits fours. My mother used to make them for us whenever she was in pie-making mode and we'd get them as an after-school snack. Today, my brother Pierre, all-grown up, a father and grandfather, still finds them irresistible.

	pie dough trimmings from the recipe on page 131	
2 tbsp	unsalted butter, softened	30 mL or 30 g
¼ cup	brown sugar	60 mL or 50 g

1. **Prepare the oven and the cookie sheet:** Place the oven rack in the middle position and preheat the oven to 375 °F (190 °C). Line a small cookie sheet with parchment paper.

2. **Shape and roll out the dough:** Make a disk with the rolled-out dough trimmings. On a floured work surface, use a floured rolling pin to roll out the disk into a thin rectangle about 8-by-10 inches (20 cm by 25 cm), by rolling from the middle outwards and lengthwise. Trim the sides and ends.

3. **Spread the filling:** Spread the butter on the dough rectangle and sprinkle the brown sugar evenly over the butter. Press down lightly on the sugar so it sticks to the butter.

4. **Roll out and shape:** Starting with one of the shorter sides of the pastry rectangle, roll tightly up to the middle and repeat with the other side. The two rolls should be the same size. Lightly press the two rolls together while slicing them into rounds about ⅜-inch (1 cm) thick. The cookie rounds should now look like palm leaves or elephant ears. Transfer to the cookie sheet, placing the slices cut side up. Adjust the shape of the slices if necessary.

5. **Bake** in the oven for 20 to 25 minutes, or until the sugar starts bubbling and the rolls are golden brown.

6. **Cool, serve and store:** Transfer to a wire rack to cool. Serve warm or at room temperature. The palmier rolls will keep at room temperature for 1 to 2 days or in the freezer for 2 to 3 months.

sweet endings
RIGHT-SIDE UP, UPSIDE-DOWN and OVER THE TOP

Apple Crisp
serves 8

Less than one hour

Why make it complicated when you can make it simple? Made with apples, pears, peaches or berries, a fruit crisp is the perfect last-minute dessert. The best apples to use are varieties that soften and keep their shape as they bake. Rosemary, a friend who's an apple crisp connoisseur, recommends using Granny Smith and Honeycrisp apples together to get the right taste and texture. In this recipe, the balance between the unsweetened fruit filling and the crisp topping comes out just right.

	CRISP TOPPING	
½ cup	unsalted butter, softened	120 mL or 115 g
1 cup	brown sugar	240 mL or 200 g
1 cup	old-fashioned rolled oats	240 mL or 90 g
1 cup	all-purpose flour	240 mL or 120 g
	APPLE FILLING	
4-5 cups	Granny Smith and Honeycrisp apples, (about half and half), peeled, cored and sliced	950 mL - 1.2 L or 520-655 g
1 tsp	ground cinnamon	5 mL

1. **Prepare the oven:** Place the oven rack in the middle position and preheat the oven to 350 °F (180 °C).

2. **Make the crisp:** In a bowl, cream the butter and the brown sugar with an electric mixer at low speed. Add the rolled oats and flour. Mix for about 1 minute, or until the mixture is in lumps the size of small peas. Reserve.

3. **Assemble:** Arrange the sliced apples in a baking dish of about 6 cups (1.4 L) and sprinkle with cinnamon. Spread the crisp topping over the apples. Use your hands to distribute it evenly and press down gently.

4. **Bake** in the oven for 25 to 30 minutes, or until the filling is bubbling at the edges and the crisp topping is golden brown.

5. **Cool and serve:** Transfer to a wire rack to cool. Serve warm. The apple crisp goes well with vanilla ice cream or plain yogourt.

6. **Store:** The apple crisp will keep in the refrigerator for 3 to 4 days or in the freezer 2 to 3 months.

Note: *This recipe is easily reduced or doubled. As a guide, for two portions, use 1 cup (240 mL or 130 g) of fruit, 2 tbsp (30 mL or 30 g) of butter, ¼ cup (60 mL or 23 g) of old-fashioned rolled oats, ¼ cup (60 mL or 30 g) of all-purpose flour, ¼ cup (60 mL or 50 g) of brown sugar and ¼ tsp (1 mL) of cinnamon.*

RASPBERRY PUDDING CAKE
SERVES 8 TO 10

A delicious dessert that tastes like a raspberry pie and practically makes itself. In my grandmother Thérèse's days, she could only make it in raspberry season, but now that there are frozen raspberries, we can make it all year around. Forewarned is forearmed: a breeze to make and gone with the wind as everyone always asks for second helpings. My nephew Laurent and his partner Leng are usually first in line.

	RASPBERRY FILLING	
6 cups or 30 oz	raspberries, fresh or frozen, unsweetened	1.4 L or 855 g
¾-1 cup	granulated sugar	180-240 mL or 150-200 g
	CAKE TOPPING	
¼ cup	unsalted butter, softened	60 mL or 56 g
½ cup	granulated sugar	120 mL or 100 g
1	large egg, beaten, at room temperature	1
1 cup	cake and pastry flour	240 mL or 120 g
2 tsp	baking powder	10 mL or 10 g
½ tsp	salt	2.5 mL or 2.5 g
2 cups less 2 tbsp	milk, 2% or whole	95 mL

1. **Prepare the oven:** Place the oven rack in the middle position and preheat the oven to 350 °F (180 °C).

2. **Make the raspberry filling:** Place the raspberries, fresh or frozen, in a large bowl and sprinkle them with sugar. Coat the fruit evenly with sugar by mixing gently. Transfer to an 8-by-12-inch (20 cm x 30 cm) baking dish. Reserve.

3. **Make the cake topping:** In a bowl, sift the flour, baking powder and salt. Reserve.

4. In another bowl, cream the butter with a wooden spoon, or an electric mixer at low speed, and gradually add the sugar and the egg. Slowly incorporate the dry ingredients while alternating with the milk, until all the ingredients are just mixed in.

5. **Drop** several spoonfuls of the batter over the fruit and spread with the back of a spoon to cover most of the surface. The batter will continue to spread while baking.

6. **Bake** in the oven for about 1 hour, or until the topping is golden brown and a toothpick inserted in the centre of the cake topping comes out clean.

7. **Cool and serve:** Transfer to a wire rack to cool. Serve warm with vanilla ice cream.

8. **Store:** The raspberry pudding cake will keep in the refrigerator for 2 to 3 days or in the freezer for 2 to 3 months.

Variations

- My grandmother made the filling with 4 cups (950 mL or 565 g) of raspberries and 1 cup (240 mL or 200 g) of sugar. I prefer more fruit and less sugar.
- Use blueberries instead of raspberries.

Food for Talk
Raspberry Pudding Cake p. 147
Please note - quantity of milk for the cake topping should
read 1/2 cup less 2 tbsp (95 ml),
(NOT 2 cups less 2 tbsp).

Date cake
WITH Brown Sugar Frosting
makes one 8-inch (20 cm) cake and serves 8 to 10

About 1 to 3 hours

There's not much to say when the words speak for themselves — dates and brown sugar. This recipe comes from my mother who made it for me when I was a teenager and who still bakes it for my birthday every year. This cake is wickedly sweet and brings back memories of my "sweet" sixteen. I enjoy it just as much now as I did then, except now it's in smaller quantities.

½ cup	unsalted butter, softened	120 mL or 115 g
1 cup	brown sugar	240 mL or 200 g
2	large eggs, at room temperature	2
1¾ cups	cake and pastry flour*	420 mL or 215 g
3 tsp	baking powder	15 mL or 15 g
½ tsp	ground cinnamon	2.5 mL
½ tsp	ground nutmeg	2.5 mL
pinch	salt	pinch
½ cup	milk, 2% or whole	120 mL
½ cup	chopped dates	120 mL or 80 g

1. **Prepare the oven and pan:** Place the oven rack in the middle position and preheat the oven to 350 °F (180 °C). Butter and flour an 8-inch (20 cm) round cake pan, or the same size Bundt pan.

2. **Make the batter:** In a large bowl, cream the butter and the brown sugar together with a wooden spoon. Add the eggs and mix until the mixture is smooth.

3. In a small bowl, sift the flour, baking powder, cinnamon, nutmeg and salt. Using a wooden spoon, gradually incorporate the dry ingredients to the butter mixture by alternating with the milk. Add the dates and mix until the ingredients are just combined. Pour the batter into the cake pan.

4. **Bake** in the oven for 35 to 45 minutes, or until the cake is cooked and a toothpick inserted in the centre comes out clean.

5. **Cool and frost:** Transfer to a wire rack to cool for 6 to 8 minutes. Turn out the cake and let cool completely on the wire rack. When the cake has cooled completely, put it on a serving plate and spread the Brown Sugar Frosting (page 151) evenly on the top and sides of the cake.

6. **Serve and store:** Serve at room temperature. The cake will keep at room temperature for 2 to 3 days or in the freezer for 2 to 3 months.

* The cake and pastry flour (1¾ cups, 420 mL or 215 g) can be replaced by 1⅓ cups (320 mL or 160 g) of all-purpose flour with ⅓ cup (80 mL or 53 g) of cornstarch.

Brown Sugar Frosting

It's not the same as Québec's beloved "sucre à la crème" but this brown sugar frosting is close enough to satisfy any sucre à la crème lover, like Marie, my husband Michel's daughter.

½ cup	unsalted butter	120 mL or 115 g
1 cup	brown sugar	240 mL or 200 g
¼ cup	milk, 2% or whole	60 mL
1¾ cups	icing sugar, sifted	420 mL or 210 g

1. In a saucepan, melt the butter over low heat. Add the brown sugar and bring to a boil while stirring for about 2 minutes or until the sugar has melted.

2. Add the milk and bring back to a boil. Remove from the heat.

3. Cool before gradually adding the sifted icing sugar. Mix until the frosting is smooth. Increase the quantity of icing sugar as needed for the frosting to be thick enough to cover the cake. The warm frosting will be a little runny but will harden as it cools.

carrot cake
WITH cream cheese frosting
makes one 2-Layer cake and serves 8 to 10

About 1 to 3 hours

In the early 80s, carrot cake was the happening cake in Toronto. Small stylish cafés like Yorkville's Just Desserts or the Brown Cow Café near Queen Street West featured it on their dessert menu. So many hours of shared confidences over pieces of carrot cake with my friends Carol or Marie! While I can't recall where the recipe comes from, I know this carrot cake is just as rich and moist as I remember it.

1 cup	brown sugar	240 mL or 200 g
1 cup	neutral-tasting vegetable oil such as sunflower oil	240 mL
3	large eggs, at room temperature	3
1⅓ cups	whole wheat flour	320 mL or 170 g
1¼ tsp	salt	6 mL or 6.25 g
1½ tsp	baking soda	7.5 mL or 9 g
1⅓ tsp	baking powder	7 mL or 6.7 g
1⅓ tsp	ground cinnamon	7 mL or 6.7 g
2 cups	shredded carrots	475 mL or 190 g
½ cup	chopped walnuts or chopped pecans	120 mL or 75 g
¼ cup	raisins	60 mL or 35 g
¼ cup	unsweetened shredded coconut	60 mL or 23 g

1. **Prepare the oven and pans:** Place the oven rack in the middle position and preheat the oven to 300 °F (150 °C). Butter two 8-inch (20 cm) round cake pans and line with parchment paper.

2. **Make the batter:** In a large bowl, mix the brown sugar with the oil. Add the eggs one at a time and mix with a wooden spoon or with an electric mixer, increasing from low to high speed, until the mixture is smooth. Reserve.

3. In another bowl, sift the flour with the salt, baking soda, baking powder and cinnamon. Gradually incorporate the dry ingredients to the wet mixture with a wooden spoon, or an electric mixer at low speed, until the ingredients are just blended in. Add the carrots, walnuts, raisins and coconut. Mix. Pour the batter equally into the cake pans.

4. **Bake** in the oven for 50 to 60 minutes, or until the cakes are cooked and a toothpick inserted in the centre comes out clean.

5. **Cool and frost:** Transfer to a wire rack to cool for 6 to 8 minutes. Turn out the cakes, remove the parchment paper and let cool completely on the wire rack. When the cakes have cooled, put one cake on a plate and spread the Cream Cheese Frosting (page 155) evenly on the top and sides of the cake. Put the second cake over the first and repeat.

6. **Serve and store:** Serve at room temperature. The cake will keep in the refrigerator for 2 to 3 days or in the freezer for 2 to 3 months.

cream cheese frosting

MAKES ICING FOR ONE 2-LAYER CAKE

In 30 minutes

4 oz	cream cheese, softened	115 g
¼ cup	unsalted butter, softened	60 mL or 56 g
3 cups	icing sugar, sifted	700 mL or 360 g
1 tbsp	pure vanilla extract, or maple syrup (optional)	15 mL

1. Cream together the cream cheese and the butter in a bowl with an electric mixer at medium speed.

2. Gradually add the sifted icing sugar and mix until the frosting is smooth. Adjust the quantity of icing sugar as needed for the frosting to be creamy enough to spread easily, and thick enough to cover the cake. Optional: flavour with vanilla or maple syrup.

UPSIDE-DOWN APRICOT CAKE
WITH VANILLA SAUCE

About 1 to 3 hours

Makes one 10-inch (25 cm) cake and serves 8 to 12

My mother adores apricots — fresh, dried, canned, in a jam — but her favourite is when they're baked up in this cake. Like a fine wine that improves with age, this cake really improves the next day when it's had a chance to soak up more of its sweet apricot nectar. Have it with vanilla sauce and experience pure pleasure.

	APRICOT TOPPING	
24-30	dried apricots	24-30
1¼ cups	water	300 mL
2 tbsp	granulated sugar	30 mL or 25 g
	CAKE BATTER	
⅓ cup	unsalted butter, softened	80 mL or 75 g
1 cup	brown sugar	240 mL or 200 g
3	large eggs, separated, at room temperature	3
1 cup	granulated sugar	240 mL or 200 g
6 tbsp	dried apricot poaching liquid from step 2	90 mL
1 cup	all-purpose flour, sifted	240 mL or 115 g
1 tsp	baking powder	5 mL or 5g

1. **Prepare the oven:** Place the oven rack in the middle position and preheat the oven to 375 °F (190 °C).

2. **Prepare the apricot topping:** Put the dried apricots in a saucepan and cover them with the water. Add the granulated sugar and bring to a boil. Simmer for about 15 minutes and remove from the heat. When the apricots have cooled, strain and reserve the poaching liquid. Split the apricots in half to make them half as thick but keeping their original round shape. They will come apart easily with your hands.

3. In a large ovenproof frying pan, about 10 or 11 inches (25 or 28 cm), melt the butter with the brown sugar over medium-low heat while mixing with a wooden spoon. When the sugar has dissolved, remove from the heat and arrange the apricots over the sugar-butter mixture, making sure they do not overlap. Reserve.

4. **Make the cake batter:** In a small bowl, sift the flour and the baking powder. Reserve.

5. In another bowl, beat the egg yolks with an electric mixer, increasing from low to high speed, until they are thick and pale. Gradually add the granulated sugar by alternating with the apricot poaching liquid. Incorporate the sifted flour until the ingredients are just mixed in. Reserve.

6. In another bowl, beat the egg whites with an electric mixer, increasing from low to high speed, until they form firm peaks*. Fold the egg whites into the cake mixture with a spatula. Pour the cake batter over the bed of apricots.

7. **Bake and cool:** Put the frying pan in the oven and bake for 25 to 30 minutes, or until the cake is cooked and a toothpick inserted in the centre comes out clean. Transfer to a wire rack to cool for 8 to 10 minutes.

8. **Transfer to a cake plate:** Run a knife around the edges of the cake to loosen it from the pan. Place a cake plate upside down on the frying pan and, while holding the plate firmly against the frying pan, flip them both over. When you remove the frying pan, the apricots are face up.

9. **Serve and store:** Serve the cake at room temperature with Vanilla Sauce (page 159). The cake will keep at room temperature for 2 to 3 days or in the freezer for 2 to 3 months.

157

vanilla sauce

MAKES ABOUT 1 CUP (240 ML) OF SAUCE, JUST RIGHT FOR ONE CAKE

In 30 minutes

If you're looking for an alternative to whipping cream or vanilla ice cream, this light velvety dessert sauce won't disappoint. In addition to the Upside-Down Apricot Cake, it pairs delightfully well with the Apple Crisp (page 145) or Raspberry Pudding Cake (page 147).

2	large eggs, at room temperature	2
3 tbsp	2% or whole milk	45 mL
1 cup	icing sugar, sifted, divided	240 mL or 120 g
1 tsp	pure vanilla extract	5 mL
1-2 tbsp	cognac, rum or sherry (optional)	15-30 mL

1. **Separate the eggs** by putting the egg yolks in one bowl and the egg whites in another.

2. **Beat the egg yolks** with an electric mixer, increasing from low to high speed, until they are thick and pale. Gradually add the milk and ½ cup (120 mL or 60 g) of the icing sugar. Mix and reserve.

3. **Beat the egg whites** with an electric mixer, increasing from low to high speed, until they form soft peaks. Add the remaining ½ cup (120 mL or 60 g) of the icing sugar and continue to beat until the egg whites form firm peaks*.

4. **Make the sauce:** With a spatula, fold the egg whites into the egg yolk mixture. Add the vanilla and flavour with cognac, rum or sherry (optional).

5. **Store and serve:** Keep the sauce in the refrigerator until ready to serve, no more than 1 or 2 days, or in the freezer for 2 to 3 months.

* To beat egg whites into firm peaks, make sure that the beaters and the bowl (glass or stainless steel) are clean and dry. The eggs should be at room temperature.

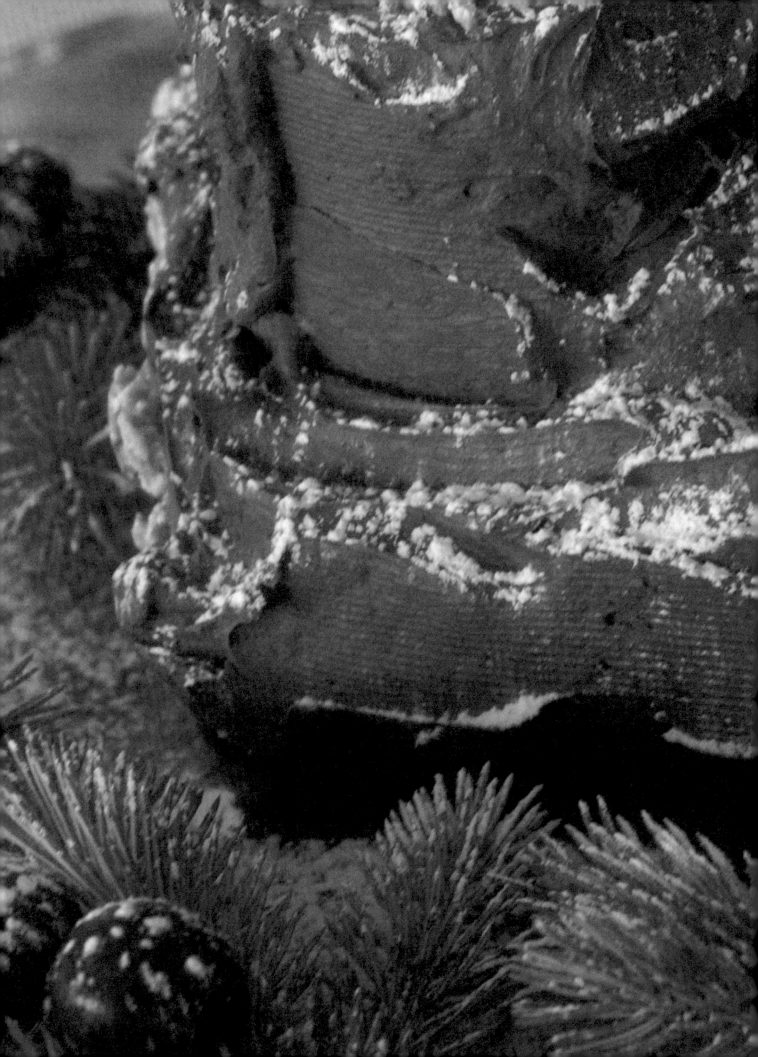

HOLIDAY DISHES
TAKE THE TIME TO REVIVE YESTERDAY'S FLAVOURS FOR TOMORROW'S MEMORIES

ANOIR LAVIOLETTE
J.-A. VEZINA, PROP.
251, BLVD LAVIOLETTE
TROIS-RIVIERES, Que.

ons Canadiens
Vézina.

s d'une livre.

c (haché moyen)
yen
ne hachées moyen

viandes séparément.

chaudron épais avec couvercle.
uter de l'eau froide par-dessus
on n'ait pas à en ajouter pendant la

ts finement hachés
de clous de girofle en poudre
de cannelle en poudre
au
d'oignon et

à feu rapide et
mps en temps.
nnements

Rincer l
cretons

Recou
genr

GranD-maman Rose's cretons

Cretons is a very Québec dish, traditionally a cold pork spread, that takes almost a whole day to make. Dating back to the late 1800s, this is my great-grandmother Delvina Marquis' recipe, made with both pork and veal, which she passed on to her nine daughters, including my grandmother Rose. Just before the Second World War, my grandfather Antoine Vézina became the owner of the Manoir Laviolette Hotel in Trois-Rivières. Look on the opposite page to see the family cretons recipe that my grandfather typed up for Rose, his wife, on the hotel letterhead.

Every year, grandmother Rose would make cretons in large quantities to feed family and friends throughout the holidays. In those days, cretons were made with "graisse de panne", or pork kidney fat, which is almost impossible to find today. A few years ago, my aunt Madeleine and her daughter Marie-Claude figured out that duck fat was a good substitute, while my aunt Monique and her daughter Renée decided they would make it without the added fat. After four generations, this family tradition (with its variations) is well enshrined, and the holidays would just not be the same without cretons on the menu. Merci, grand-maman Rose!

2 lb	medium ground pork*	900 g
2 lb	medium ground veal*	900 g
1 lb	duck fat**	454 g
2	medium onions, finely chopped	2
½ tsp or more	ground cloves	2.5 mL or more
¼ tsp or more	ground cinnamon	1 mL or more
	salt and pepper	
	onion salt (optional)	
	celery salt (optional)	

1. Prepare the mixture: In a large stockpot, combine the pork, veal, duck fat and onions. Cover generously with cold water up to about 1 inch (2.5cm) above the meat. For about 10 minutes, use a wooden spoon to break up the meat. Add the cloves, cinnamon, salt and pepper. Optional: add onion salt and celery salt. Mix.

2. Cook: Bring to a boil over medium-high heat while stirring constantly to prevent the meat from sticking to the bottom. Reduce the heat to medium-low, cover and simmer for 6 to 7 hours. During that time, stir frequently and taste to adjust the seasoning. Remove from the heat and cool for 30 minutes.

3. Pot and chill: Put the cretons in small bowls or crockpots. Let cool completely. Wrap the potted cretons in plastic to prevent them from drying. Put in the refrigerator overnight.

4. Serve with toasted bread or crackers.

5. Store: The cretons will keep in the refrigerator for about 1 week or in the freezer for 2 to 3 months.

* *Ask the butcher to grind the pork and veal separately for you. This way, the quantities will be equal for each, something grandmother Rose insisted on.*

** *Reduce the amount of fat, if desired.*

OLD-FASHIONED TOURTIÈRES

MAKES THREE DOUBLE-CRUST 9-INCH (23 CM) PIES

More than 3 hours

Tourtières, or meat pies, can be made any time of the year but they're really a traditional holiday dish in Québec. Many people think that the word "tourtière" comes from the word "tourte", the wild North American pigeon that had been used in these pies until it became extinct. In fact, it comes from "tourtière" as in the name of the container in which it was cooked which then became the name of its contents.

In Québec, the recipes for tourtières are often family recipes handed down from one generation to the next. My mother followed her mother-in-law Rose's recipe for the meat filling but preferred her own recipe for the pie crust.

	MEAT FILLING	
2½ lb	medium ground pork	1.1 kg
2½ lb	medium ground veal	1.1 kg
2½ cups	cold water	595 mL
3	medium onions, finely chopped	2
½ tsp or more	ground cloves	2.5 mL or more
¼ tsp or more	ground cinnamon	1 mL or more
	salt and pepper	
	PASTRY*	
6	rolled-out 11-inch (28 cm) dough circles	6
1	egg yolk beaten with 1 tbsp (15 mL) of cold water	1

1. **Make meat filling:** In a Dutch oven, combine the pork and the veal. Cover with cold water. For about 10 minutes, use a wooden spoon to break up the meat. Add the onions, clove, cinnamon, salt and pepper. Mix. Bring to a boil over medium-high heat while stirring constantly to prevent the meat from sticking to the bottom. Reduce the heat to medium-low, cover and simmer for 3 to 4 hours. During that time, stir frequently and taste to adjust the seasoning. Remove from the heat and cool completely, about 2 hours.

2. **Prepare the oven:** Place the oven rack in the bottom position and preheat the oven to 375 °F (190 °C).

3. **Assemble the pies:** Line one of the 9-inch (23 cm) pie plates with one rolled-out dough circle. (Refer to the Classic Pie Dough recipe on page 131 for how to do this). Put ⅓ of the meat in the pie plate. Cover the meat with a second dough circle, allowing it to hang evenly over the edges by about ¾ inch (2 cm). Use a knife to trim the edges. Tuck the overhanging dough underneath itself, and then rest the rim on the lip of the pie plate. To flute the rim, use the index of one hand and the thumb and index of the other hand to make ridges perpendicular to the pie plate. Repeat to assemble the next two meat pies.**

4. **Vent and baste top crust:** With a knife, cut a few openings on the top crust of each tourtière to let the steam escape during cooking. With a pastry brush, baste the crust with the egg wash, but not the rim.

5. **Bake** in the oven for 40 to 50 minutes, or until the crust is golden brown.

6. **Cool and serve:** Transfer to a wire rack to cool. If needed, warm up before serving. The tourtières are delicious with marinated beets or fruit ketchup.

7. **Store:** The tourtières will keep in the refrigerator for about 1 week or in the freezer for 2 to 3 months.

* *Use the recipe on page 131 or buy six ready-made rolled-out 11-inch (28 cm) dough circles at a grocery store.*
** *The tourtière in the picture on the page opposite is made in a deep-dish pie plate.*

Tante Élise's Baked Beans
with Salt Pork
serves 10 to 12

More than 3 hours

It's hard to get excited about an everyday dish like beans and pork until you've tasted the homemade version. They're a food tradition all year round in Québec, but especially between the holiday season in winter and sugar shack season in the spring. The sweetening agent may be maple syrup, molasses or brown sugar, or a combination of these. This is tante Élise's recipe and she makes it with both molasses and brown sugar. The rich aroma of slow-cooked baked beans in the kitchen is as comforting as the dish itself. It is well worth the 15 to 20 hours from start to finish.

4 cups or 2 lb	small dry white beans, such as navy beans	950 mL or 900 g
½ lb	lean salt pork, in ¼-inch (6 mm) dice	225 g
1	large onion, chopped	1
½ cup	molasses	120 mL
1 tsp	dry mustard	5 mL or 3 g
¼ cup	brown sugar	60 mL or 45 g
2 tsp	apple cider vinegar	10 mL
¼ cup	ketchup*	60 mL
1 tsp	salt	5 mL
¼ tsp	pepper	1 mL

1. **Soak the beans:** Wash the beans thoroughly, rinse and drain. Put the beans in a large bowl and cover generously with lukewarm water. Cover the bowl with a tea towel and soak at room temperature for 5 to 6 hours, or overnight. Keep the beans in their soaking water, now rich in iron and vitamins. Reserve for step 3.

2. **Prepare the oven:** Place the oven rack in the bottom position and preheat the oven to 250 °F (120 °C).

3. **Cook the beans:** In a stockpot of 16 cups (4 L), bring the beans and the bean-soaking water to a boil. Reduce the heat to medium and simmer uncovered for 20 minutes. Skim off the foam and set aside.

4. **Blanch the salt pork** in a saucepan of boiling water for about 1 minute. Remove from the heat, drain and rinse.

5. **Assemble:** In a baked bean pot**, combine the beans and the soaking liquid, the salt pork, and all the remaining ingredients. The beans should be covered with about ½-inch (1.25 cm) of liquid; if not, add water. Mix and cover.

6. **Bake** in the oven for 7 to 8 hours, stirring about once an hour. If needed, add water to keep the beans from drying out. After about 6 hours, uncover the pot to taste and adjust the seasoning. Continue baking uncovered for 1 to 1½ hours, or until the beans are tender and have a nice dark colour.

7. **Cool, serve and store:** Let cool for about 5 minutes. Taste and adjust the seasoning before serving. The beans are delicious with ham and a tomato salad. They will keep in the refrigerator for about 1 week or in the freezer for 5 to 6 months.

* Tante Élise uses Heinz ketchup.
** If you don't have a baked bean pot, use a Dutch oven like the ones made by Le Creuset.

ROaST TURKEY WITH STUFFING

serves 12

This is a tale of two turkeys. On Christmas day, when my paternal and maternal grandparents were still alive, we would visit my grandmother Rose for lunch, and later in the day head off to my grandmother Thérèse for dinner. We had the full turkey feast at both places and the recipes were as different as their cooks. Over the last several years, my mother has been hosting her sisters Marie and Élise and their families for Christmas lunch, with two turkeys to feed 25 to 30 people. Aunt Élise used to prepare both turkeys, but lately she's been sharing the task with my mother. Both follow my grandmother Thérèse's recipe, each in their own way. This is my mother's version.

16-18 lb	fresh turkey and giblets	7.25-8.2 kg
1	carrot, roughly chopped	1
1	celery stalk with leaves, roughly chopped	1
1	onion, cut in half	1
1	bay leaf	1
	salt and pepper	
1	lemon, cut in half	1
1 tbsp	olive oil	15 mL
2-3 tbsp	Madeira wine	30-45 mL

1. **Make the giblet broth:*** Remove the giblet bag from the turkey. In a small saucepan, combine the giblets, carrot, celery, onion and bay leaf. Cover with water and season with salt and pepper. Bring to a boil, cover and simmer over low heat for 2 hours. Strain and set the broth aside.

2. **Prepare the oven:** Place the oven rack in the bottom position and preheat the oven to 350 °F (180 °C).

3. **Prepare and stuff the turkey:** Rinse the turkey inside and out under cold running water. Dry thoroughly with paper towels. Place the turkey in a large roasting pan. Rub the inside and outside of the turkey with the lemon halves. Generously season the inside of the turkey with salt and pepper. Tuck the wings behind the back of the turkey. Fill the body and neck cavities loosely with the stuffing (page 171) as the stuffing will expand as it cooks. To keep the stuffing inside, pull the neck skin taut under the turkey backbone, and close the body cavity by overlapping the skin and keeping it tightly in place with turkey skewers or by sewing it shut. Brush the turkey with the olive oil. Tie the two drumsticks together with kitchen twine and cover with aluminum foil to prevent them from burning while cooking.

4. **Cook extra stuffing:** Transfer any unused stuffing into a baking dish, cover, and cook for about 45 minutes next to the turkey.

5. **Roast the turkey:** Allowing a cooking time of 20 minutes per lb (454 g), cook in the oven from 5 hours and 20 minutes to 6 hours, or until the turkey is golden brown and cooked. As it roasts, baste with the reserved broth from time to time. About 30 minutes before the end of the cooking time, remove the aluminum foil from the drumsticks to let them turn golden brown. A stuffed turkey is cooked when a meat thermometer inserted in the thickest part of the inner thigh, without touching the bone, reads 180 °F (82 °C), a thermometer inserted in the stuffing placed in the cavity reads 165 °F (74 °C) and the juices run clear when the turkey is pierced.

6. **Let the turkey rest:** Transfer the turkey to a serving dish. Cover loosely with aluminum foil and let the turkey rest for 30 minutes for the juices to settle into the meat.

7. **Make the gravy:** Put the roasting pan on the stovetop and deglaze it by scraping with a wooden spoon. Add some broth as necessary. Simmer over low heat for 10 minutes. Taste and adjust the seasoning. Add Madeira wine to taste and stir. Pour into a gravy boat.

8. **Carve and serve:** Carve the turkey and serve with the gravy and stuffing. Turkey pairs well with green peas and cranberry jelly.

9. **Store:** The carved turkey will keep in the refrigerator for 4 to 5 days or in the freezer for 3 to 6 months.

* Prepare in advance and refrigerate for 3 to 5 days, or use homemade or packaged chicken broth.

STUFFING
serves 12

Less than one hour

To stuff or not to stuff? For my niece Lara, a turkey is not worth eating if there is no stuffing. Every year, we double up the recipe so that everyone can have as much as they want. My recipe is my mother's recipe, with a modern addition of green apple and pine nuts to give it some freshness and crunch.

8 cups	white bread, in ¾ inch (2 cm) cubes, with or without the crust	1.9 L or 265 g
1 cup	salted or unsalted butter	240 mL or 225 g
1	large onion, chopped	1
1½ cups	chopped celery stalks	350 mL or 195 g
¼ cup	chopped fresh curly parsley	60 mL or 8 g
pinch	dried summer savory	pinch
	salt and pepper	
1	Granny Smith apple, peeled, cored and cut into ½-inch (1.25 cm) dice (optional)	1
¼ cup	pine nuts, toasted (optional)	60 mL or 40 g

1. **Prepare the oven:** Place the oven rack in the middle position and preheat the oven to 250 °F (120 °C).

2. **Make the croutons:** Put the bread cubes on 2 sheet pans and bake for about 20 minutes, or until the bread cubes are barely toasted, but dried and crisp. Stir the cubes during baking. Do not skip this step as properly dried out bread cubes are key to the success of the stuffing. Reserve.

3. **Cook the vegetables:** In a large frying pan, melt the butter and cook the onions, celery and parsley over medium heat for 8 to 10 minutes, or until the vegetables are softened. Season with summer savory, salt and pepper to taste. Mix and reserve.

4. **Assemble:** In a large bowl, combine the bread cubes and vegetables. Toss well so that the bread cubes have absorbed the butter. Optional: Add the apple and the toasted pine nuts. Mix.

5. **Refrigerate** the stuffing no more than 1 to 2 days before stuffing the turkey. If a turkey is stuffed in advance, there is a risk of developing bacteria inside it.

YULE LOG

December 23rd is a very special day for me. This is the day when I get together with my cherished childhood friends Marie and Dorothée to make six Yule Logs. We take turns in each other's kitchen and we bring our ingredients and baking tools. As soon as we put on our aprons, we transform ourselves into Santa's pastry elves. We follow Margo Oliver's December 1974 recipe to the letter. Over the years, we have perfected our assembly line process: Marie makes the rolled cakes, I prepare the coffee buttercream and Dorothée finishes off with the chocolate frosting. We chat away to the sound of the electric mixers and, at the end of the day, we return to our respective homes, covered with flour dust, triumphantly carrying our decorated Yule Logs, and smiling from ear to ear.

STEP 1: ROLLED CAKE

3	large eggs	3
1 cup	granulated sugar	240 mL or 200 g
5 tbsp	water	75 mL
1 tsp	pure vanilla extract	5 mL
1 cup	all-purpose flour, sifted	240 mL or 115 g
1 tsp	baking powder	5 mL or 5 g
¼ tsp	salt	1 mL or 1 g
¼ cup or more	icing sugar	60 mL or 30 g, or more

1. **Prepare the oven and pan:** Place the oven rack in the middle position and preheat the oven to 375 °F (190 °C). Butter a 10-by-15-inch (25 cm by 38 cm) cake roll pan and line with parchment paper.

2. **Prepare the egg mixture:** In a bowl, beat the eggs with an electric mixer at high speed for 5 minutes, or until the eggs are thick and pale. Gradually add the sugar and beat well after each addition. Add the water and vanilla while beating.

3. **Make the batter:** In a small bowl, sift the flour with the baking powder and salt, add to the egg mixture and incorporate until the mixture is smooth. Pour the mixture into the cake roll pan and spread evenly.

4. **Bake** in the oven for 12 to 15 minutes, or until the cake is lightly golden and light pressure with a finger on the centre of the cake does not leave a print.

5. **Cool and roll the cake:** Transfer the pan to a wire rack to cool for 10 to 12 minutes. On a work surface, lay flat a clean dish towel. The towel should be at least the size of the cake, and slightly damp. Sift the icing sugar as you sprinkle it generously over the entire surface of the towel. Turn out the cake, remove the parchment paper, and carefully place it right side up on the towel. Starting with the shorter end of the cake, loosely roll up the cake together with the dish towel. The icing sugar will prevent the cake from sticking to the rolled-up towel and make it easier to unroll when you are ready to decorate the log. Reserve.

STEP 2: coffee Buttercream

1 tbsp	instant coffee granules	15 mL or 4 g
1 tbsp	boiling water	15 mL
5	large egg yolks*	5
⅓ cup	water	80 mL
½ cup	granulated sugar	120 mL or 100 g
1 cup	unsalted butter, in 1-inch (2.5 cm) cubes, softened	240 mL or 225 g
¼ tsp	pure vanilla extract	1 mL

1. **Prepare the coffee:** In a small bowl, dissolve the coffee granules in the boiling water and cool. Reserve.

2. **Prepare the yolks:** In a bowl, beat the egg yolks with an electric mixer, increasing from low to high speed, until they are thick and pale. Reserve.

3. **Prepare the sugar syrup:** In a small saucepan, combine the water and sugar. Warm up over low heat and stir for a few minutes until the sugar has dissolved. Increase the heat to medium-high and bring to a boil. Continue boiling without stirring until the temperature reaches 230 °F (106 °C) on a candy thermometer, or until the syrup reaches the thread stage, leaving threads on the tip of a fork. Remove from the heat immediately

4. **Make the buttercream:** Without waiting pour the syrup slowly into the egg yolks while beating with the electric mixer. Continue to beat at medium speed until the mixture is lukewarm. Add the butter, one cube at a time, and continue beating after each addition. If too much butter is put in at once or if it is too cold, the buttercream will separate. Add the cooled coffee and vanilla while beating. The buttercream should be smooth and look like whipped butter. If the buttercream is too soft, put it in the refrigerator for a few minutes. Reserve for Step 4 or refrigerate for 3 to 5 days.

The unused egg whites can be used to make meringues, if desired.

STEP 3: CHOCOLATE FROSTING

¼ cup	unsalted butter, softened	60 mL or 55 g
2 cups	icing sugar, sifted	475 mL or 240 g
2 tbsp	15% cream	30 mL
1 tsp	pure vanilla extract	5 mL
2-4 oz	unsweetened dark chocolate (100% cocoa)	60-115 g

1. **Melt the chocolate:** In the top part of a double boiler, melt the chocolate over simmering water. Stir until it is smooth. Alternatively, melt the chocolate in the micro-wave for 60 to 90 seconds at high power.

2. **Make the frosting:** In a bowl, cream the butter with an electric mixer at medium speed and incorporate the icing sugar. Little by little, pour in the cream and mix well. Add the vanilla and the melted chocolate and continue mixing until the frosting is completely smooth.

3. **Store:** The frosting can be prepared in advance and refrigerated for about 1 week. Bring to room temperature before frosting the log.

STEP 4: FILLING AND ROLLING THE LOG

1. Fill with buttercream: On a clean work surface, unroll the towel-wrapped rolled-up cake and lay it perfectly flat. Carefully remove the towel. With a spatula, spread the coffee buttercream over the entire surface of the cake, while reserving about ¼ cup (60 mL) to decorate the frosted log.

2. Roll the cake loosely, starting from one of the short ends of the cake. The cake is now in the shape of a log.

3. Trim the log: At each end of the cake, cut off a diagonal wedge about 1-inch (2.5 cm) thick at the widest part. These will serve as knots on the log. Set each wedge on top of the log and use some of the chocolate frosting to hold them in place. Transfer the log to a serving plate.

STEP 5: FROSTING AND DECORATING THE LOG

1. Spread the chocolate frosting over the entire log as well as the sides of the knots with a spatula, trying to imitate the bark of a real log. Do not cover the ends of the log or the top of the knots with the chocolate frosting.

2. Spread the coffee buttercream on the ends of the log and on the top of the knots. With a fork, make concentric circles on the buttercream to imitate wood grain.

3. Decorate the log with bits of real spruce branches and fresh cranberries, and sprinkle icing sugar all over to suggest fallen snow.

4. Store: The log will keep in the refrigerator for about 1 week or in the freezer for 2 to 3 months.

* To make more than one log, repeat the single recipe, one log at a time.

GranD-maman THérèSe's
PLUM PUDDING WITH RUM Sauce

More than 3 hours

makes 1 PLUM PUDDING anD serves 12 TO 16

This sweet ending to a Christmas meal goes all the way back to medieval England when plum meant any dried fruit. Starting in the early 1930s, and for over 50 years, plum pudding was my grandmother Thérèse's specialty, and her recipe had plenty of dried fruit. After she died, my aunts Marie and Élise took over the making of the pudding and these days the torch is being passed on to my cousin Louise and her daughter Laurence, my cousin Paule, and my sister Catherine. On Christmas Day, as this elegant dessert occupies centre stage on the table, aunt Élise sets it on fire with rum while we sit in silence watching the dancing flames. All together we clap our hands in gratitude for this brief ceremonial blessing of the "holy day."

1 cup	currants	240 mL or 140 g
½ cup	brown rum, divided	120 mL
¼ cup	candied angelica*	60 mL or 47 g
½ cup	candied lemon*	120 mL or 95 g
½ cup	candied citron*	120 mL or 95 g
½ cup	candied orange*	120 mL or 95 g
3-4	apples, Cortland or Gala, peeled and cored	3-4
1 cup	dates	240 mL or 160 g
1 cup	dried figs	240 mL or 160 g
1 cup	light sultana raisins	240 mL or 140 g
1 cup	dark sultana raisins	240 mL or 140 g
1 cup	breadcrumbs	240 mL or 150 g
2 cups or 12 oz	ground beef suet**	475 mL or 340 g
1	lemon, zested	1
2 cups	brown sugar	475 mL or 400g
1 ½ cups	all-purpose flour	350 mL or 185 g
1 tsp	baking powder	5 mL or 5 g
1 tsp	salt	5 mL or 5 g
5	large eggs, beaten	5
½ tsp	ground cloves	2.5 mL
½ tsp	ground cinnamon	2.5 mL
2 tsp	fine white sugar	10 mL or 10 g
⅓ cup	brown rum to flame the pudding	80 mL

1. **Prepare the currants:** In a small bowl, soak the currants in ¼ cup (60 mL) of rum for 1 hour. Reserve.

2. **Prepare the remaining fruit:** Cut the candied fruits (angelica, lemon, citron, and orange), apples, dates, and figs into ³⁄₁₆-inch (5 mm) dice.

3. **Make the batter:** In a large stoneware bowl, combine the rum-macerated currants and their liquid, candied fruits, apples, dates and figs, and both kinds of raisins. Add the breadcrumbs, suet, lemon zest and brown sugar. Mix.

4. Sift the flour with the baking powder and salt, then add to the batter. Add the beaten eggs, the remaining

¼ cup (60 mL) of rum, cloves and cinnamon. Using your hands, work all the ingredients together until they are fully incorporated.

5. **Prepare and fill the mould:** Very generously butter an 8-cup (2 L) steam pudding mould***. Transfer the pudding batter and fill the mould three-quarters of the way up the sides. Press the pudding tightly against the inside walls of the mould so that it takes on its shape. Cover the mould with 2 layers of wax paper, letting the paper hang down the outer sides of the mould. Tie the paper with a kitchen string around the mould to keep it in place. Set the lid over the paper to cover and close the mould.

6. **Steam:** Put a small wire rack on the bottom of a stockpot large enough to easily contain the pudding mould. Place the mould on the wire rack. Fill the stockpot with water three-quarters of the way up the sides of the mould. Cover and bring to a boil. Reduce the heat to low for the water to simmer. Continue cooking covered for 3 hours.

7. **Make the rum sauce:** While the pudding is steaming, prepare the rum sauce. See page 179.

8. **Cool and refrigerate:** Remove the stockpot from the heat and transfer the mould to a wire rack to cool. After 5 to 8 minutes, remove the cover and the wax paper, and turn out the pudding. Place the pudding on a wire rack to cool completely. Wrap the pudding in plastic and then aluminum foil. Keep in the refrigerator and remove a few hours before serving so that it comes to room temperature.

9. **Serve:** Remove the aluminum foil and the plastic wrap. Place the plum pudding on a cake plate and sprinkle with fine white sugar. Bring the pudding to where it will be served.

10. **Flame the pudding:** Heat the rum over medium heat in a small saucepan for a few minutes. Immediately bring it to the plum pudding already set on the table in front of your guests. Pour the hot rum over the pudding. Carefully use a match to set the rum-drenched pudding on fire. Enjoy the short-lived show as the flames will very quickly die down. Serve the flamed plum pudding with the rum sauce.

11. **Store:** Before or after being flamed, the plum pudding will keep in the refrigerator for 3 to 6 months or in the freezer for 1 to 2 years.

---

*   The candied fruit (angelica, lemon, citron and orange) can be difficult to find. Adjust the mix of candied fruit with what you have while keeping the total quantity at 1¾ cups (420 mL or 330 g), or buy packaged mixed candied fruit at grocery stores.

**   Ground beef suet can be found at butcher shops.

*** A steam pudding mould is essential for the recipe, so why not treat yourself? Buy a large 8-cup (2 L) steam pudding mould, 2 medium moulds of 4 cups (1 L), or 4 small moulds of 2 cups (500 mL).

Rum Sauce

½ cup	unsalted butter	120 mL or 115 g
1 cup	fine white sugar	240 mL or 200 g
1	large egg, beaten	1
3 tbsp	brown rum	45 mL

1. **Make the sauce:** In the upper part of a double boiler, melt the butter over simmering water. Add the sugar and mix with a wooden spoon. Add the egg and cook for about 15 minutes while stirring to dissolve the sugar. Remove from the heat, add the rum, and mix. Let cool and put in the refrigerator.

2. **Reheat and serve:** About 5 minutes before serving the plum pudding, reheat the sauce in a saucepan over low heat. Transfer to a sauce boat.

3. **Store:** The sauce will keep in the refrigerator for 3 to 4 weeks or in the freezer for 4 to 6 months.

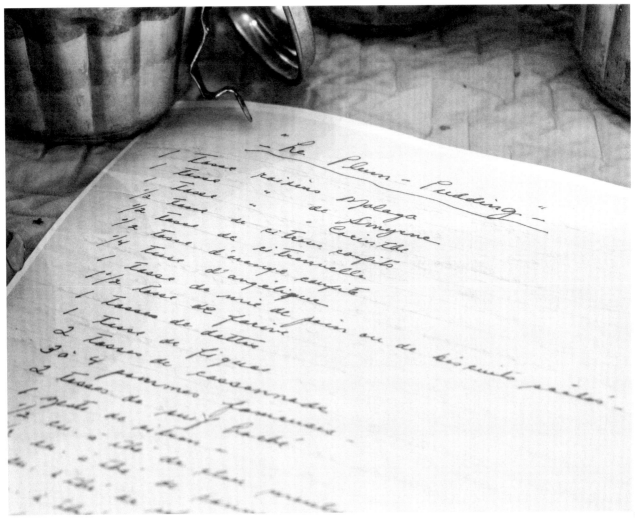

Selected Bibliography

BRUNO, Diana. *Lexique français-anglais de la cuisine et de la restauration.* Montréal, Centre collégial de développement de matériel didactique, Collège Maisonneuve. Février 2019.

Tableau de conversions. https://www.recettesquebecoises.com

Guide 101 sur la congélation. https://www.ricardocuisine.com

INDEX

C

D

D

E

F

G